history
of
Mexico

Stella M. González

PANORAMA EDITORIAL, S.A.

Carmen G. Blázquez

history
of
Mexico

from pre-hispanic times to the
present day

Front cover:
"Hidalgo". Mural painting
Government Palace. Guadalajara, Jalisco.

"La Trinchera". National
High School, Mexico, City.
José Clemente Orozco
I.N.B.A.

Seventh edition in English: 1985
© Panorama Editorial, S.A.
   Leibnitz 31, Col. Anzures
   11590 México, D.F.

PANORAMA SERIES
   Under the direction of:
   Federico Santiago E.

Translated by:
   David Castledine

Drawing by:
   José Narro

Printed in Mexico
Impreso en México

ISBN-968-38-0000-9 English
ISBN-968-38-0035-1 Spanish
ISBN-968-38-0033-5 French
ISBN-968-38-0034-3 Germany

index

American Man

There are various theories as to the origin of American man. One of them states that he came from Asia, reaching America via the Bering Strait or the Aleutian Islands. Another says that American man started out from Polynesia and arrived in America by means of the Pacific currents running from the south to America. According to yet another, he originated in Egypt, crossing the Atlantic from Africa to America.

The most likely of these theories is the first, since it has the most evidence to support it at present. American man, not aboriginal, traveled from Asia on foot across the Bering Strait, possibly during the ice-age when a frozen bridge stretched between Asia and America.

The History of Mexico can be studied under three major headings, the two first ones each ending in a crisis of struggle. The headings are Native Mexico, Colonial Mexico and Independent Mexico. The crises are the Spanish Conquest and the War of Independence.

*"he came from Asia,
reaching America via the
Bering Strait..."*

Native Mexico

The culture of American man in his first stage is very primitive. The most ancient remains found in Mexico are those of Tepexpan man (8000 B.C.). It was in this remote period that the Archaic and Olmec cultures developed.

The Archaic Cultures are located on various sites in the Valley of Mexico: Tlatilco, Zacatenco, Ticomán and principally Copilco, where tombs of a primitive type with human remains and stone and clay objects were found. Notable is the number of female figures discovered in the most representative sites of the Copilco culture, these being in fact what typify Copilco. Cuicuilco is another site belonging to this cultural phase, and presents constructions half-buried under lava from the Xitle volcano. The principal remaining monument is a circular pyramid, with a base 135 meters in diameter and some 25 centimeters high.

Traces of the Archaic culture are found away from Mexico City: in the southeast of the Republic, the so-called complex "Q" or Pre-Maya culture, El Opeño and Chupí-cuaro in Michoacán.

A large part of Mexico, together with the countries of Central America constitute what is known as Mesoamerica. Throughout this vast territory we find various cultural zones, such as the Olmec, that flourished in the States of Veracruz and Tabasco; the Nahua, situated in the center of Mesoamerica and embracing the valley of Mexico and its closest surrounding area; the Mixtec-Zapotec, that developed in the State of Oaxaca, and the Maya area, comprising the peninsula of Yucatán and the States of Tabasco and Chiapas in Mexico as well as Guatemala, El Salvador and part of Honduras.

As can be seen, Mesoamerica is an extensive zone where numerous groups developed, different one from the other but interchanging cultural elements and influencing each other in various ways.

Elements of flora and fauna are for the most part common to all Mesoamerica. Corn was the most important grain, as it formed the basis of American man's whole diet. To this can be added beans, squash, chili and both culinary and medicinal herbs. Cotton, agave, tobacco and cacao were also grown, but on a lesser scale.

As for fauna, domestic animals were the turkey and a breed of dog kept for fattening. Bees, the source of honey, were also highly valued by the natives. The native diet, in itself lean and austere, was supplemented with wild animals that differed according to the region. Towards the mid 16th century, cooking among the Mesoamericans was advanced and savory.

It is not to be thought that Mesoamerica became a single unit in a short time; on the contrary, it needed approximately 3000 years to form itself into a cultural area.

During this time, each group developing within it created its own individual history, although all had a common stem.

There were cities in Mesoamerica, but not all of them reached urban perfection, and some more than others still have the appearance of cities. In the Maya area, organization is not so clear, but in the valleys of the high plateau on the other hand, a well-developed sense of city planning is evident.

The majority of the cities were organized in the following manner: religious area (the temples); administrative area, (the palaces) and the living areas, (housing). The greatest care was taken in the construction of the temples, that were built on a pyramidal base and set among other admirable stone structures.

The common elements of all Mesoamerican architecture were the sloping wall and vertical wall (talud y tablero) and relief as decoration. Stucco was commonly used to cover facades, walls and even sculptures. Brick was rarely employed, as even the humblest buildings were of adobe.

In addition to the constructions mentioned above there was the one used for the most popular sport among the tribes of Mesoamerica: the ball court. It was in the form of a letter I, and may be of various dimensions but always for the same sport.

Art in Mesoamerica shows a wide range of different forms, from the most delicate to the coarsest. Remains of this art can be found in bas reliefs, carvings and murals as well as in articles of personal decoration, such as ear-ornaments, necklaces, bracelets, pectorals, etc.

Mesoamerican art was also enriched with all the feather-work articles and with the abundant pottery, both ceremonial and domestic that has been left in different forms and various colors. Later, metal was added as an artistic medium, as metalworking was born in Mesoamerica possibly around the year 900, and it is after this date that we find art treasures in gold, made by a special technique called the lost wax process.

The weapons used by the Mesoamericans can also be considered as expressions of their art, since they were ingenious and refined. Among the most common ones are the Atlatl, a sort of spear thrower, the club and a kind of wooden sword set with razor-sharp pieces of obsidian.

In one way or another, Mesoamerican man has left us evidence of a well-developed artistic sense, a simple and lucid expression of his soul molded into the objects he created.

The family was both the base and pivot of the society and the towns of Mesoamerica. One family lived grouped with others in centers called "calpulli", named "barrios" (communities) by the Spaniards when they arrived. Gradually men began to acquire a definite place in these groups, so creating the social classes that were basically two: the nobles and the common people. The former occupied the most important positions both in religious and military spheres, and so had the power in their hands. The latter formed the town proper, that is to say, those who made up the calpulli. It was to these two classes that the different ranks that existed belonged, and so we find priests, nobles, warriors, merchants, farmers and common men (macehualli). Clearly, in 16th-century Mesoamerica, there already existed a system that indicates a nation leaving behind the characteristics of tribal organization.

In its political structure, we see that there is always one nation that dominates others and this is how the Empire arises, a system of government by one tribe that in dominating others exacts tribute and demands rights. The Empire in Mesoamerica gives rise to a very generalized relationship between tribes and men.

The native was religious, and we find expressions of this in the rich ceremonial that existed among the original populations of Mesoamerica as well as in pottery and in the abstract concepts they manipulated. In Mesoamerica we find numerous figurines, mainly female, that were symbols of fertility and agriculture. Similar gods were worshiped throughout Mesoamerica. We know for instance that the cults of the god of water, of the earth or of the moon were very widespread, which leads us to the conclusion that the gods venerated were in fact the same, but with different names.

Little is known about the rites, but we can be sure that in these and in religious ceremonies certain animals, and even humans, were sacrificed. The latter practice is intimately connected with war, since the Mesoamericans believed that the prisoner of war was the sacrifice most acceptable to the god, which explains the effort made to take prisoners in battle. However, war did not have religious ends, its object was always commercial and imperialist.

The group that cultivated religion was that of the priests, and the members of this privileged class enjoyed great prestige because of their wide scientific knowledge. They were masters of writing, handled the calendar through their knowledge of astronomy, cured illness with their medical lore, and were in charge of higher education because of their scholarship. All this learning was a valuable, help in influencing and in holding a high degree of power over the population.

Writing, first known in Mesoamerica in the middle of the first millennium B.C., was an effective instrument in cultural progress through stone inscriptions. A little later appeared mural paintings, pottery and the codices, pictorical books that tell us of both the historical and religious world of Mesoamerican man. In these we learn details about the gods, the calendar and the most important events that took place at the time they were being produced.

We know that two calendars were in use in Mesoamerica, one of 365 days, called the solar calendar, and another of 260 days, the divinatory. By combining the two, a cycle of 52 years was arrived at that could be compared to what we now call a century.

Among the Olmecs and the Mayas there was also a more exact system for expressing the date, known as the Long Count, that ran from a mythical date in the past. The zero was used in this Long Count, otherwise it would not have been possible to express the high numbers, up to million of years, that these groups registered, definite proof in itself that they knew and used the zero.

Astronomy is intimately linked to this mathematical precision, the exact calculations being made after observing the movement of certain stars, and especially of the planet Venus whose appearance and disappearance gave rise to a rich mystic concept, and it was perhaps from this cycle that arose the concepts of duality that the Mesoamericans were familiar with, such as day and night, life and death, masculine and feminine, good and evil, and several other ideas of polarity.

The above gives us a general idea of the civilization of Mesoamerica as a cultural area, but at the same time shows us on comparing it with other cultures, that the elements described above are not peculiar to Mesoamerica but were shared with peoples on the northern and southern frontiers, and with other more distant civilizations.

Olmec Civilization

Varied and rich civilizations developed in Mexico at different periods; these we shall examine one by one.

The Olmec civilization is considered the mother culture since it was the one that influenced later ones such as Teotihuacan, Maya and Zapotec. The Olmec culture is known by various names: the culture of the rubber region, the culture of the Jaguar god and also as the culture of the sculptures. All these names are derived from actual characteristic features of this civilization.

Our knowledge of the Olmecs comes from the traces they have left behind, since nothing is known of their origins. The principal Olmec centers were La Venta and Tres Zapotes in the north of the State of Tabasco, and San Lorenzo in the south of the State of Veracruz. It was mainly from these three centers that Olmec civilization exerted its influence on later-developing groups and cultures.

The Olmec area is situated throughout the basin of the river Papaloapan, that is to say it comprises the northern part of the State of Tabasco, and the southern part of Veracruz. The area over which the traces of this great culture are scattered covers 1,200 sq. km.

From the first millennium B.C. the Olmecs show a great artistic talent in their pottery that consisted of numerous well-fired figurines in orange clay. The jaguar and childlike seated figures are the main and characteristic products of this culture.

Other distinguishing features of Olmec art are colossal human heads, stylizations of the Jaguar god, and the Olmec mouth that resembles the jaws of the jaguar, the divine hieratic symbol of this culture. Another sculpture, also considered classic of this culture is the Wrestler (El Luchador) or ball-game player, so called from the attitude of the figure, that skillfully reflects realism in stone. This was discovered at Uxpanapan, Veracruz.

Let us examine the main places where Olmec civilization flourished.

San Lorenzo is where the most ancient archeological remains of this culture can be observed. Located between the Coatzacoalcos and Chiquito rivers, it is believed to date back to 300 B.C. The architectural complex of San Lorenzo is built on an artificial platform 50 meters high, and is bounded on three sides by ravines made by the Olmecs, perhaps for purposes of defence. Up to now, seven stone human heads of enormous proportions have been discovered on this site. The stone monuments that are believed to have existed were mutilated and in some cases buried, and those that have been found indicate that there was once a wealth of stone sculptures here.

La Venta, some 15 kms. from the coast of the Gulf of Mexico, is the most representative site of the Olmec culture. La Venta, extending over 5.22 sq. km., lies on an island

formed by the Tonalá river that meanders along the Veracruz and Tabasco border in a marshy region dotted with
numerous islands.

The archeological remains uncovered consist of ceremonial buildings that form an irregular rectangle with the
main pyramid. Both north and south of this lie monuments
and some mounds. The large pyramid of an irregular shape,
was built by accumulating clay. It is some 128 meters in
diameter, 31.40 m. high, and the whole mass is calculated
at some 100,000 cu. meters.

The remains at La Venta show us that the Olmecs
planned and organized their buildings carefully and that in
them they used large amounts of clay due to the absence
of stone in this region. La Venta is perhaps the prototype
for the ceremonial precincts of later cultures.

Another example of the Olmec culture is Tres Zapotes
stretching for 3 km. along the right bank of the Hueyapan
river. The buildings left by the population of this region
consist of two fairly low terraces and some higher buildings.
The constructions form a well planned square from where
50 mounds making up part of the site can be seen. Tres
Zapotes has not been sufficiently explored for the degree
of culture it reached to be assessed.

Teotihuacan

Teotihuacan means "Place of the Gods" or place where those who die become gods. The first interpretation can perhaps be explained by the fact that 'Teotihuacan' means the city of Teul (god); the second is because it was where the great lords were buried, who were immediately regarded as gods.

Located in the northeast of the valley of Mexico, it covers one tenth of the 600 km. square area.

The settlement of Teotihuacan seems to have begun between 400 B.C. and the first millennium B.C. and it was at Teotihuacan in 2 B.C., that the most important cultural development in central Mexico began.

At first a ceremonial center surrounded by small farming settlements, Teotihuacan grew as it incorporated the neighboring villages and at the same time as it expanded, underwent constant cultural changes. Teotihuacan is the classic city of the Mesoamerican world, showing already an advanced urban culture and admirable organization.

Teotihuacan appears to have been well organized from the very beginning, with monumental temples and palaces, living quarters grouped in blocks, paved streets and an underground drainage system.

The city went through four distinct phases. The first is devoid of external influence. In the second, the influence of the Gulf culture infiltrated through the cult of the Jaguar-Serpent. In the third phase, Olmec influence is very strong and apparent, revealing itself fully in pottery and architecture. At that moment Teotihuacan reached its maximum splendor, both artistic and political. Finally, in its fourth stage Teotihuacan declined due to influence from outside that caused ethnic and religious problems at its heart. The end of Teotihuacan came with Chichimec invasions in the mid 9th century. The conquerors mutilated the expressions of the overthrown religion, leaving clear proof of a high degree of change in the temples and edifices of the great city.

The axis of the constructions at Teotihuacan is the causeway running north-south called the "Avenue of the Dead". The first building is the Pyramid of the Moon, followed by the Palace of Butterflies, the Temple of Agriculture, the Square of the Columns, the colossal Pyramid of the Sun, the Temple of Tláloc, the underground chambers and finally the Citadel. At the side of this last monument stands the Pyramid of Quetzalcóatl and Tláloc with masterly sculptures of these gods.

These are the remains of a city full of life and color, the prototype of advanced Mesoamerican culture that entered its period of decadence when it was not able to integrate the new elements, arriving from the valley of Mexico, either racially or religiously.

Monte Albán ("White Mountain") is a site standing some 500 meters above the mean level of the valley of Oaxaca. All the constructions raised by the members of this civilization are located on the upper part of the hill. Monte Albán, just like Teotihuacan, imposed itself on the farming peoples of the valley and became the Zapotec capital, managing to conserve its strength and dominion for a long time. Its grandiose buildings and monuments also contribute to the resemblance to the sacred city of the valley of Mexico. The oldest examples of writing in Mesoamerican have been discovered at Monte Albán.

Studies and exploration have shown that Monte Albán went through various cultural phases. These are really four, although often said to be five, but the last or fifth phase belongs rather to Mixtec culture.

The Classic Monte Albán culture began in the 8th century B.C., and indications of its art and socio-religious life exist in various constructions, figures and paintings.

The human figure appears in various attitudes reminiscent of a dancer. The influence received from the Olmecs can be seen in the human faces as well as in glyphs and lines used for numeration.

The pottery of Monte Albán was of good quality, burnished, decorated with incised geometrical designs and usually gray.

Each different period of Monte Albán experienced innovations that modified the concepts of the period immediately prior to it. These changes were due to the influence received sometimes from Chiapas and Guatemala, sometimes from Teotihuacan, until at last decadence set in, noticeable in the inferior quality of the buildings dating from 900 A.D. onward. This was when Monte Albán ceased to be the most important political and religious center of the Zapotecs. After its period of decadence, it fell into the hands of the Mixtecs, who made the top of the hill into a necropolis. Only a few tombs have been excavated, the most interesting being No. 104 and No. 105 that have various paintings inside. Tomb No. 7 is notable for the priceless treasure of gold objects found there.

The Mixtecs are believed to have occupied Mitla before the Aztecs conquered it at the end of the 15th century. We know that Mitla was the burial place of great Zapotec lords and perhaps a center of pilgrimage. The architectural decoration of Mitla is rich and varied, and the perfectly interlaced Greek key patterns are a feast of decoration, displaying a highly esthetic harmony.

All the buildings at Mitla are fairly low, and are symmetrically arranged to form an impressive complex.

Let us take a closer look at the Mixtecs. We know that "Mixteca" in the Nahuatl language means inhabitant of the country in the clouds. This name may have been given to the people because of the mountain region where they lived, often shrouded in great clouds. The Mixtec region is in the northeast of the state of Oaxaca.

The Mixtecs distinguished themselves as excellent goldsmiths, potters and painters of codices. In these activities they achieved real works of art that even nowadays can cause wonder. The Mixtec codices, dealing with the calendar, history, astronomy or genealogy, are the best among those of the native peoples of the valley of Mexico. Through them we can begin to appreciate the history of the Mixtec people and the governors of the different domains into which Mixtecapan was divided, namely Tilantongo, Achiutla, Tlaxiaco, Tuxtepec and Coixtlahuaca. As can be seen, the Mixtecs never enjoyed political unity because of constant domestic struggles among themselves, that prevented any one domain from gaining supremacy over the others. A definite and clear cultural cohesion did however exist among the Mixtecs.

The period generally known as Monte Albán V is simply another, purely Mixtec cultural phase, which seems to be the same in the case of Yagul, a site near Mitla.

The Mixtecs expanded thanks to the power they held among the tribes of the valley of Oaxaca and the imperialist pressure exerted on them by the Aztecs towards the middle of the 15th century.

The Mayas

The Mayas are another great and powerful culture in Meso-america. This civilization developed in Mexico, Guatemala, Honduras and El Salvador. In Mexico it embraced the States of Tabasco, Campeche, Yucatán and Quintana Roo.

The Yucatán peninsula is the area that tells us most about this culture through its numerous monumental buildings. Yucatán is a very hot region, with very few lakes, lagoons or rivers because its permeable limestone crust allows water to filter through and become deposited in the subsoil in natural caves called cenotes.

The cultural growth of the Maya civilization began with a formative period when its characteristic features took shape and became unified. The altars and carved stelae belong to this period, when writing makes its first appearance and social classes gradually become clearly defined. The calendar is proof of the Maya's advanced knowledge of mathematics and astronomy.

The pottery, stone carvings and tombs are also a sign of a technological advance among the Mayas. The so-called Maya vault or false arch made possible the rubblework roofing used in both civil and religious buildings. This architectural invention totally changed Maya constructions, making them peerless models.

This period, from the beginning of the Christian era to the year 300, gave rise to the splendor of the only Classic Maya period.

In the Classic period we see an economic boom, a greater cohesion among the population and an extraordinary demographic growth, and remarkable new cultivation techniques were used on a wide area comprising the neglected agricultural lands. All these elements indicate the social and economic development of Mayas of the priod.

Society supported in its midst a parasite class composed of nobles and priests who ensured social union so that the numerous collective works could be carried out. Thanks to this labor force it was possible to raise the richly decorated buildings of ceremonial centers where the size of this collective effort can be appreciated. Social stratification was accentuated by the power wielded by the ruling class, that used its influence not only as a political but also economic and religious control.

The Classic period ends in the 10th century, leaving behind a galaxy of important monuments such as those forming the centers of Uaxactun, Copán and Tikal in Central America, Dzibilchaltun, Tulum and Kabah in the Yucatán peninsula; Palenque and Bonampak in the jungle of Chiapas, Chichen Itza, Uxmal and Mayapán rose later, towards 1300 A.D. in the Yucatán peninsula as representatives of the Maya-Toltec fusion.

In this region, the Classic period came to an end with the invasion of Toltec groups who succeeded in imposing their rule on the Maya population of the peninsula. Their power was not only political, but also cultural and religious, and can be clearly seen in the architecture of their monuments and the cult of Quetzalcóatl. As a result of this influence together with the Classic elements of Maya culture a new style emerged representative of this cultural and religious fusion.

Let us examine some notable Classic Maya sites more closely.

Tikal is the most important center in the Guatemalan Petén. Its architecture is of grandiose proportions and perhaps the most spectacular in all the Maya country. The roof combs with which these builders finished off their constructions are distinctive.

In Copán (Honduras) and Quiriguá (Guatemala) we do not find, as in the Petén, either tall pyramids or temples with roof combs, but there is however a similarity to the monuments of Yucatán in the masks of the Rain god placed at the corners of the temples.

Piedras Negras, Palenque and Bonampak among others belong to the region of the Usumacinta river. In these centers of culture the Mayas gave more importance to historical events, proved by the various stelae relating the lives of their leaders or chiefs. Religious themes are almost absent from the artistic expressions of this zone. The sculpture that flourished in this region, especially at Piedras Negras, Yaxchilán and Bonampak was full of movement and surprisingly realistic. The murals of Bonampak are also outstanding examples in the Maya area.

Three styles of architecture flourished in the Yucatán peninsula that take their names from the region where they developed, namely Puuc, Chenes and Rio Bec.

The Puuc style grew up on various sites in the so-called low sierra (puuc) in the southwest of the state of Yucatán. This style is characterized by the use of Greek key patterns, serpent motifs, inset colonettes and stone masks for the decoration of facades, and stucco facing is an essential feature; Uxmal, Kabah, Sayil and Labná, among others are examples of the Puuc style.

The Chenes style is characterized by the excessive decoration of facades, on which no part remains untouched. A typical feature of the facades is a main entrance formed by the gaping mouth of a monster probably representing the Rain god. The influence of this style can be seen in the Puuc region. The name Chenes is applied to a region in the central part of the State of Campeche, where the names of many towns end in the Maya "chen", meaning well.

The Rio Bec style was formed in the south of the central part of the peninsula, that is to say in southern Campeche and in Quintana Roo near the border with Guatemala. Buildings crowned with towers are characteristic of this style of architecture, that is very similar to the Chenes style in its heavily decorated facades.

When the Classic Maya period came to an end (10th century) some buildings — those at Uxmal, to be exact — underwent changes. Examples of this are the ball court and the Quadrangle of the Nuns. Quetzalcóatl was integrated into the decoration of the latter building in the form of a plumed serpent called Kukulkán by the Mayas.

Warriors in clothes similar to those worn by Toltec soldiers are added to the decoration of the buildings at Kabah, and we also see them later on the pillars at Chichén Itzá. Also at Chichén Itzá the construction of a circular observatory indicates the presence of the Toltecs, since this

*"gave rise to
the splendor of
the Maya culture. . ."*

type of structure was not used by the Mayas prior to the Classic period. Some time after the Classic period Chichén Itzá was the seat of Toltec government in Yucatán.

The Classic Maya period came to an end in the 10th century, leaving behind brilliant monuments to its culture and gradually initiating the period of decline of the Mayas of the peninsula that lasted until the day when the Spaniards arrived on the coasts of Yucatán.

In addition to the preceding Classic cultures, there were in Mexico highly important local cultures such as Xochicalco (some 30 kms. from Cuernavaca) Tecas (in the States of Nayarit, Jalisco, Colima and Michoacán) and Tajín, also known as the Totonac culture. We shall look at this last and most important one.

The Olmec, Maya and Huastec cultures as well as that of Tajín are known as the civilizations of the Gulf of Mexico.

The Tajín culture is found in the State of Veracruz and was influenced to a greater or lesser degree by the culture of Teotihuacan and especially by that of the Mayas. The characteristic features of the Tajín culture are hollow clay figurines made in molds whose smiling faces show remarkable simplicity and realism. The area is also rich in Yokes, classic items of this culture that are objects carved in hard stone, usually green. Of the same material are the so-called Axes and Palms, which are carved and finely polished, some bearing carved faces and designs, and are believed to have been used in ceremonies.

Near Papantla stands a monument of the Tajín culture considered to be the most important relic on the Gulf coast. It is an enormous seven storeyed pyramid measuring 35 m. along each side of its base. At each level run series of niches, the purpose of which is not known but which give the pyramid of El Tajín its name: the Pyramid of the Niches.

This culture was developing throughout the Classic period and during its life received and assimilated the influence of the Toltecs, Mixtecs and later of the Aztecs.

Chichimecs and Toltecs

The name Chichimec, says Fray Bernardino de Sahagún, was the one given to the tribes that appeared in the Valley of Mexico under the leadership of Mixcoatl, and is a direct reference to their former nomadic life. Since the Chichimecs founded a great city called Tollan, the name of Toltecs was later given to them, alluding to this notable event.

Before they founded this metropolis and were known by the name of Toltecs, these tribes reconnoitered the greater part of the valley of Mexico to select a place in which to settle and at the same time build and exercise control over the peoples they had encountered on their travels. They crossed the valley of Toluca, passed near Teotihuacan and Acolman and finally established themselves for a considerable time on the Cerro de la Estrella, south of the lakes of the valley of Mexico. It was from here that their struggle to dominate began, that culminated in the erection of the great city of Tula-Xicocotitlan.

Chichimecs and Toltecs

The name Chichimec, says Fray Bernardino de Sahagún, was the one given to the tribes that appeared in the Valley of Mexico under the leadership of Mixcoatl, and is a direct reference to their former nomadic life. Since the Chichimecs founded a great city called Tollan, the name of Toltecs was later given to them, alluding to this notable event.

Before they founded this metropolis and were known by the name of Toltecs, these tribes reconnoitered the greater part of the valley of Mexico to select a place in which to settle and at the same time build and exercise control over the peoples they had encountered on their travels. They crossed the valley of Toluca, passed near Teotihuacan and Acolman and finally established themselves for a considerable time on the Cerro de la Estrella, south of the lakes of the valley of Mexico. It was from here that their struggle to dominate began, that culminated in the erection of the great city of Tula-Xicocotitlan.

The Toltecs are thought to have settled permanently at Tula-Xicocotitlan in the 10th century, but not before being influenced by certain peoples such as those living at Xochicalco and the Xicalango Olmecs, who at that time were absolute masters of Cholula.

Mixcoatl, in his desire to extend his domain, came into contact with the deeply rooted cultures of other tribes, that logically exerted a direct civilizing influence.

Mixcoatl was succeeded on the throne by his son Topiltzin Quetzalcóatl, and it was at this time that the Chichimecs experienced a profound change and the golden age of this civilization began, an age that later resulted in the Toltecs being held in high esteem by all the peoples of Mesoamerica for their culture. Among the principal admirers of the Toltecs were the Mexicas and the inhabitants of Texcoco.

Looking at the historical evidence and the archeological remains of this epoch, it is easy to see that while Tula-Xicocotitlan flourished, Mesoamerican culture spread to its greatest extent. It stretched along the northern frontiers and Toltec influence was felt as far as Tamaulipas (Soto la Marina river) and even the region of La Quemada in Zacatecas and the area surrounding the Fuerte river in Sinaloa. When Tula fell and the Toltecs were dispersed, they spread to the most distant regions of central, south and southwest Mesoamerica. This influence is attested by the investigator Jiménez Moreno with these words: "From an archeological point of view, the monuments of Chichén Itzá provide the standard by which to judge things Toltec, because here it is easy to distinguish the Toltec elements, foreign additions to the preexisting Maya culture. If these same extraneous elements, which Maya sources attribute to the Toltecs, are compared to similar ones in central Mexico, immediate affinities with Tula in the State of Hidalgo become apparent."

The characteristic creations that the Toltecs demonstrated to their contemporaries are various and a large part of them can still be seen nowadays in the archeological remains left by this people.

Among the most outstanding ones must be mentioned a style of architecture characterized by grandiose complexes, where decoration and detail are secondary. We also find vestibules or porticoes supported by lines of columns and, beyond the portico, large rooms built perhaps for cultural or ceremonial purposes.

The main architectural features are columns in the shape of a serpent with its head on the ground and its body pointing upward.

The rings for the ball-game and columns like caryatids, together with standard holders and chacmools are yet other forms that attest to the advanced art of the Toltecs.

The bas reliefs of the Toltec civilization are often in polychrome. In many friezes there are processions of warriors, representations of plumed serpents interspersed with the human figure of Topiltzin Quetzalcóatl who is on a background of a plumed serpent or eagle devouring hearts or else figures of tigers or coyotes. All these figures are to be seen on the vertical wall (tablero) of the Pyramid of Tlahuizcalpantecuhtli, which has a double frieze. In this same temple the atlantes or giants of Tula are noteworthy, monumental stone statues of warriors that have become the symbol of Tula.

The pottery made by the Toltecs is known as Mazapa, the name of a village near Teotihuacan, and is characterized by its decoration of thin lines, the orange color and the metallic sheen (lead glaze).

*"the Atlantes or giants of **Tula**
are noteworthy,
monumental stone statues..."*

The Toltecs in one way or another exerted influence on a large area of Mesoamerica, leaving cultural traces in Michoacán, Guerrero, Oaxaca, Veracruz, Tabasco and Maya country.

Because of invasions by other tribes, internal political troubles and migrations, the Toltecs declined and abandoned the region of Tula which was taken over by other peoples, thus originating the beginning of another change in the political, cultural and ethnic frame of Mesoamerica.

Mexicas or Aztecs

This tribe of Indian Mexico was not native to the center of the country and yet, by the 16th century it was the Aztecs who had achieved the greatest cultural and political advancement in this area.

From the 12th to the 14th century they put all their efforts into finding somewhere to settle. They set out from the north of Mexico, from a place called Aztlán and in the course of constant wanderings arrived first at Chapultepec, then at Culhuacán and later, in 1325, at a place called Mexico or Tenochtitlan.

Little is known about the period when they were in Aztlán, neither what the place was like nor where it was located. It would be very helpful for the history of Mexico to localize where it lay in order to trace from there the points that the Aztecs touched in their daring, constant pilgrimage.

The Mexicas, at the time they settled in Tenochtitlan, certainly possessed a purely Mesoamerican culture, acquired not by stages in their migrations, but in their place of origin. It is probable therefore that Aztlán was located within Mesoamerica.

Arriving in the valley of Mexico, the Aztecs found three kingdoms distinguishing themselves in culture and power over all the Lake Texcoco area: Atzcapotzalco, Culhuacán and Coatlinchan. The Mexicas submitted to the Tepanecas of Atzcapotzalco, and payed them tribute for nearly a century.

A few decades after the Aztecs had established themselves, an internal struggle between the three kingdoms arose. There were political changes and bloody battles in which the Aztecs took part as warriors, since they were the mercenaries the Tepanecas counted on in their expeditions of conquest. As a result of this role, the Aztecs became experts in warfare and above all came to realize the extent of their own courage and battle prowess. This knowledge would help them later to create the wide empire they formed with other native tribes.

The Aztec monarchy began in 1376, but it was not until the time of the fourth king, Izcoatl that the Mexicas became independent from the Tepanecas. The fifth king, Moctezuma I, founded the Aztec empire. He reigned until 1469 and during this time extended his power as far as Veracruz and Oaxaca. He organized the city of Tenochtitlan and gave it elegant buildings erected under the supervision of the architects of Chalco. He replaced the old huts with stone buildings and made Tenochtitlan a well-planned, flourishing and beautifully constructed city.

Moctezuma II reigned from 1502 until Cortés arrived in the city of Tenochtitlan. It was during this period that the Mexica territory reached its maximum extension, and their power and splendor their greatest height, although Tenochtitlan itself covered only 13 sq. km. The city solved its social

*"the fifth king
Moctezuma I, founded
the Aztec empire..."*

and economic problems in an organized way that commands respect. Lands were divided into private, public and communal property, thus balancing the economic status of the people.

One of the most important activities of the Mexicas was commerce that was often combined with politics and it was common to find spies and ambassadors called Tlanamacani among the merchants.

Trade ranged from the most simple — the sale of feathers and clothes made of agave fiber — to the most elaborate — the sale of jade and turquoise objects, gold jewelry and cotton clothes.

As for education, Tenochtitlan could boast of three centers: the Calmecac, where the nobles were educated, the Cuicalco, where the priests studied and the Tepochcalli where warriors were trained. The Calmecac, according to Sahagún, was one of the 78 buildings surrounded by a wall that made a structural frame for the great temple, standing in the center of the city.

The religion of the Aztecs was polytheistic and their gods include Huitzilopochtli, considered the principal guardian of the city and god of war, Tláloc, the god of water and Quetzalcóatl the god of wind. The Mexicas expected this last god to return. All these gods were represented in stone and considered principal subjects of sculpture and monumental art.

Also worthy of mention is the famous Aztec calendar, no other than the stone of the Sun, as this is the symbol appearing in the center of the great stone where four glyphs represent the four preceding cycles (or 'suns') of Aztec history. This center is surrounded by a circle of twenty symbols, representing the twenty days of the month. All this is encircled by symbols of stars and sunrays, in their turn surrounded by two immense fire serpents representing day and night that are the final frame of the design.

In spite of their advanced culture, the Mexica were not able to overcome the Spaniards with their weapons, boats and horses, that for the native mind were unknown and undreamt of. The unfamiliarity of these elements, combined with the legend of the return of Quetzalcóatl, was one of the main reasons for the ease with which the Aztecs were conquered in 1521.

Western Mexico

Mesoamerica has been divided into areas and then into subareas. Western Mexico was one of these subareas and includes various states, the most important being Guerrero, Michoacán, Guanajuato and Sinaloa.

The West is saturated with influence from the cultural worlds of central and northern Mexico. If we compare this culture with the civilization of the center, Oaxaca and Maya country, we see that the latter are remarkably advanced, while the former shows poverty in all fields of culture. The reason for this lies perhaps in the milieu in which the Western populations developed their various cultural expressions. They were unable to organize themselves into a politico-religious and social unit with firm bases.

We also notice in this area the absence of large constructions and almost total lack of Classic elements in all the native architecture. Most of the constructions are rudimentary, and rarely covered with stucco. The stone sculptures are well defined but do not achieve the standard required by Classic art. The West has neither codices nor its own writing system, its religious world is poor in gods and consequently great ceremonial temples were not built. The West is a cultural section of Mesoamerica that did not flourish sufficiently to leave its mark on native Mexico, but it did however have its importance as many cultural advances in Mesoamerica originated from there.

If we remember that the Olmec culture, mother of Mesoamerican civilization, was born in the States of Tabasco and Veracruz, we realize the enormous distance between these and the West, and this is one of the reasons why this subarea was not influenced by the advanced cultures.

We shall now deal with the most important Western cultures. The one that developed in Colima was a culture rich in pottery recreating a whole world of warriors, members of society and various expressions of pain that reveal different illnesses in the human figures of clay. Dogs (of a breed fattened for eating) are also well-known features of this pottery. The archeological sites are few and not very outstanding but do make up a wide and well-defined area.

Noteworthy places where numerous clay objects were found include Los Alcaraces and El Chamal.

The culture that developed a few kilometers from the city of Zamora, Michoacán, is known as El Opeño. Clay figures in which the influence of Zacatenco can be seen are a prominent feature of this culture also. Tombs and pottery go together and in fact are the only representatives of this local cuture.

The culture of Chupícuaro in Guanajuato is characterized by the same poverty of architectural elements that marks Western Mexico. Its pottery is however plentiful and distinctive.

Tarascans

The name Tarascos was mistakenly given to this people by the Spaniards who did not understand what the natives were saying to them in the Purépecha language. It is more correct to call them Michuacas or Purépechas.

Purépecha territory includes the States of Michoacán, Guerrero, Colima, Jalisco, Guanajuato and part of the State of Mexico. This group seems to be of Nahua origin, and to have penetrated the area from Guanajuato, conquering in turn Zacapu, Uayameo and other settlements near Lake Pátzcuaro. They began to found city states such as Tzintzuntzan and Pátzcuaro. These were governed by Tariácuri and after his death by his sons, but not with the same ability as their father. In these circumstances, Tzintzuntzan became the capital of the Purépecha Kindgom until 1528, the year in which the Spaniards defeated Zincicha.

The art and architecture of this culture is poor perhaps because it was influenced by the Western region. The greatest example of its ceremonial achitecture is in the Yácatas of

Tzintzuntzan. This group is located on the lower slopes of the Yahuarato hill, and is composed of a large artificial terrace and various units arranged at intervals, adapted to the topography of the area. At the center of the site is a great stairway up to the platform on which the Yácatas were built whose ground plan was a combination of a rectangle and a circle. The bases were built up in tiers of volcanic stone or unbonded stone slabs in piles of four, and thus rose the constructions connected with this people's death and funeral rites. The Purépecha buildings are poor, simple and austere.

We know little about the Michuacas because they had no hieroglyphic writing and therefore left no written history. The sources of information are their pottery, the 'Relación de Michoacán' by an unknown author and a pre-Cortesian Nahua document known as the Lienzo de Jucutacato. These, together with the Yácatas show us the degree of development and the modest achievements of this culture.

The Conquest

The Conquest of New Spain finds its ultimate instigation in two highly important historical events. The first was the fall of Constantinople, on May 29, 1453. When the city passed into the hands of the Turks, the land and sea routes for trade with Orient were closed, and so many people searched for ways to reach it other than the traditional ones.

Among these explorers of new routes was the Genoan, Christopher Columbus, who, helped by the friars and the Queen of Spain's treasurer, Don Luis de Santangel, managed to obtain funds and the authorization of the Spanish Crown to undertake a voyage full of hope and surprises. America was discovered as a result of this venture, that is the second historical foundation.

Ferdinand of Aragon and Isabella of Castile were rejoicing at having ended the almost eight-century-old struggle against the Moors with the capture of Granada on January 2, 1492. Three months later Columbus presented himself before them with his project, the monarchs gave their approval and the explorer weighed anchor at the port of Palos on August 3, 1492.

On October 12 of the same year Columbus discovered San Salvador (Watling Island in the Bahamas, then called Guanahaní), and later Cuba, Juana Island and Hispaniola (La Isla Española). He then returned to Barcelona where he was received by Ferdinand and Isabella. The discoverer of America died in Valladolid in 1506.

Hispaniola and Cuba then became the bases from which other expeditions set out with the hope of expanding the territories of the Spanish Crown.

In 1500 the governor of Cuba, Diego de Velázquez, concerned himself with extending Spanish dominion to other areas, and it was with this aim that expeditions towards Yucatán and México left Cuba. The first, commanded by Hernández de Córdoba, left in 1517, then in 1518 one under Juan de Grijalva, and the third was led by Cortés. The first expedition reached Yucatán, the second penetrated into the bay of Veracruz and got as far as Pánuco, the third conquered Tenochtitlan, the political heart of native Mexico.

Cortés was determined to conquer the territories with or without the help of Velázquez, and so established himself on the mainland, founding Villa Rica de la Vera Cruz. From here he became aware of the splendor of the Aztec empire and the enormous power of the king, Moctezuma II. Moctezuma and Cortés were watchful of each other's movements since the King wished the Spaniard to leave Mexico, and Cortés on his part wanted to conquer the Aztec empire. The tactics of conquest were planned: first, Cortés sent to Spain two of his captains who were to inform the sovereign of the events and obtain permission to conquer and colonize the newly discovered lands. Afterwards he decided to take

Tenochtitlan and set out in that direction on August 15, 1519.

Cortés left from Cempoala, allied himself with native tribes oppressed by the Aztecs, and massacred those such as the Cholultecs, who betrayed him or opposed his plans. He obtained peacefully the submission of Moctezuma and several other lords of the valley of Mexico.

The arrival of Pánfilo de Narváez, a Spanish captain sent by Velázquez to punish Cortés for insubordination, prompted the conquistador to leave for Veracruz and confront Narváez. He left the Spanish troops in Tenochtitlan under the command of Pedro de Alvarado, who in a moment of panic caused a massacre of natives in the Great Temple. This led to the disorganized and hasty flight of the Spaniards, while the incensed Mexica attacked them violently.

Cortés on his return from Veracruz, was met with this unpleasant new development and began to organize the withdrawal of his men. This retreat from Tenochtitlan is known to history as "La Noche Triste" (The Sad Night). After this, it seemed that all the Spaniards had done in the city had been for nothing, but they tenaciously organized a reconquest six months later.

Cuitláhuac, who was then acting as emperor died in a smallpox epidemic.

He was succeeded by Cuauhtémoc who strove unsuccessfully to repulse the invaders.

The Spaniards besieged Tenochtitlan, the emperor Cuauhtémoc tried to escape in a canoe but was taken prisoner. With the king captured, victory was easier for the conquistadors, the city of Tenochtitlan fell into the hands of Cortés, and the magnificent power of the native world came to an end.

"the first expedition reached Yucatán,
the second penetrated
into the bay of Veracruz..."

Cortés found support with Charles V of Spain, who recognized his work of conquest and granted him the title of Governor and Captain General of New Spain. The remaining native lords were gradually brought under the influence of the Conquest, sometimes violently and sometimes peacefully, but there is no doubt these lords helped the spread of Spanish authority.

One part of Maya country, Yucatán, was the only area not directly or indirectly conquered by Cortés. The other provinces were overcome by him or his captains.

In Yucatán it was the three men all by the name of Francisco de Montejo who independently of Cortés, completed the great picture of the conquest of New Spain. The same thing happened in the northwest, where it was Nuño de Guzmán who conquered the region.

Yucatán was conquered in the years 1527-1542. Montejo the father began it by penetrating the east of the peninsula, but failed. The second attempt was made by the same Montejo ("El Adelantado") and his son. They set out from Tabasco but were also unsuccessful by this route, due to the belligerence of the Mayas and the lack of financial aid from outside to continue the struggle. The third and final attempt during which Yucatán was conquered was made by Montejo the younger ("El Mozo") and Montejo the nephew. They planned the conquest to begin from Campeche. When they were already in the midst of their campaign they received help in the form of supplies and men from the elder Montejo who at that time governed Chiapas.

Thanks to this, the capital of Yucatán could be founded on January 6, 1542, with the name of Nuestra Señora de la Encarnación de Mérida. In this same year Montejo the younger and his cousin defeated the Cocomes of Sotuta and the Cupules of Conil and Chauaca.

The conquest of Yucatán culminated in the foundation of Valladolid, in the region of the Cupules, and that of Salamanca in the province of Uaymil-Chetumal. However, although Yucatán was already conquered, the Indians continued to resist for many years.

The northwest was conquered in stages by Nuño de Guzmán, firstly between 1529 and 1531, and secondly in 1541 and 1542. The second stage was a military campaign organized by Viceroy Mendoza against the dangerous uprising of Caxcana. Nuño de Guzmán's ambition was to surpass and obscure the glories of Cortés, and to this end he wished to take control of all the north and its rich kingdoms that according to the current rumors existed.

The poverty of these northern lands, in addition to the ambition and criminal conduct of the conquistador greatly reduced the merit of the conquest of the northwest. However, shining out against this dark period is the founding of the province of New Galicia.

This was carried out in two stages spanning 7 years. The first step was conquest in 1531 and the second, organization up to 1536. In the following years there were uprisings for different reasons, but they were all put down by the Spaniards and New Galicia was once and for all subdued, with its capital at Compostela.

The history of the conquest of the north is confused but we know that both New Spain and New Galicia tried to expand, settling places nearby, such as Querétaro, Guanajuato, San Luis Potosí and Zacatecas.

The Spaniards conquered other regions, creating the provinces of New Biscay, New Mexico, New Santander, Nayarit and New León. In circumstances sometimes adverse to growth, these provinces gradually became defined and found their place in the mosaic of conquests in the north of New Spain.

When the Spaniards found minerals in the north of Mexico, mining centers grew up that were always asking for settlers. This was how new population centers, such as Zacatecas (1548), Santa Fé de Guanajuato (1554) and San Luis Potosí (1592) rose.

Zacatecas was founded by Juan de Tolosa, who discovered mineral deposits. Later in order to exploit the mines, he associated with Diego de Ibarra, Cristóbal de Oñate and Baltazar Temiño de Buñuelos.

In 1562 Francisco de Ibarra was named governor of New Biscay, and organized the province admirably. In 1566 he explored Sinaloa, Sonora and southern Chihuahua. At this time, Sinaloa was uninhabited and abandoned; Francisco de Ibarra settled the region and incorporated it into New Biscay, whereas it had formerly belonged to New Galicia.

In 1580, Don Luis de Carvajal arrived from Spain with a royal warrant dated June 14, 1570 to settle the New Kingdom of León, which was to stretch 200 leagues north and the same number west of the Pánuco river. This territory would include part of northern New Galicia and part of New Biscay. The venture was unsuccessful, Carvajal was taken prisoner and later forgotten as a conquistador.

In 1596, captain Diego de Montemayor made the attempt to form and organize the New Kingdom of León. He began by resettling the town of San Luis; later, on September 20 of the same year, with twelve inhabitants of Saltillo, he founded Nuestra Señora de Monterrey.

Coahuila was founded thanks to the Franciscan, Juan de Larios, who created the missions of Mapimí, San Lorenzo, San Pedro and Cuatro Ciénegas, and also to Captain

*"Moctezuma II and Cortés
were watchful
of each other's movements. . ."*

Antonio Barcárcel, who was helped in his struggle by the neighboring authorities of Saltillo.

In 1679 the king decreed that Coahuila should depend on the Viceroyalty. Alonso de León was named first governor in 1687, and in 1689 founded the capital of Coahuila at Santiago de la Monclova and began the settling of Texas. This same governor also established the mission of San Francisco de las Texas in 1690, on the banks of the Noches river.

New Toledo, or Nayarit, was conquered in 1722. The colonization of New Santander or Tamaulipas was carried out in a period of 9 years (1746-1755) by the Count of Revillagigedo, Don José de Escandón. He took to Tamaulipas families from Spain and Tlaxcala, who by means of continuous work and sacrifice succeeded in establishing a normal rhythm of life in New Santander.

In the conquest of North of Mexico, an important factor was the existence of a dream created in the imagination of the century: the seven cities. This legend cost many famous knights their lives as they went in search of something that did not exist: seven cities, rich in gold and precious stones.

It was a slave belonging to Nuño de Guzmán who first mentioned the cities in 1530. He said that they were as big as Mexico City, fabulously rich in silver and lay far off in the extreme north.

In 1536, when Nuño de Guzmán was in Culiacán, his companions heard marvelous tales of one of these cities, called Quivira. The stories were told by four men who had been shipwrecked coming to Mexico with Pánfilo de Narváez from Spain in 1527, and had lived with the Indians of the North for 9 years.

On another occasion, Viceroy Mendoza commissioned the Franciscan Marcos de Niza to investigate the matter.

This priest returned from the North in 1539, and gave exaggerated descriptions and marvelous but false news, painting a picture of a Cíbola richer even than Mexico or Peru.

With all these tales, interest in the cities grew, and a large number of captains wished to conquer them. The Crown gave permission to no-one except Viceroy Mendoza, who immediately sent 300 men to make a search. This expedition, in 1540, was led by the governor of New Galicia, Francisco Vázquez Coronado. They reached Cíbola (now Hawikuh, New Mexico) and took the city after an hour's fighting. The soldiers were immediately disillusioned, for instead of magnificent buildings decorated with precious stones, they found miserable tumbledown houses of stone and adobe. The only remaining inhabitants were poorly dressed, some covering themselves with buffalo (cíbolo) hides.

Quivira was an even greater disappointment. The precise site of the town has still not been located; some writers say that it was in Nebraska and others, in Texas. In 1542 Coronado returned to Mexico City and reported that what they had found was very different from what had been believed for many years. It is true that they did not discover the famous riches, but on the other hand reconnaissance work important for the geographical knowledge of the North of New Spain was done.

Pedro de Tovar journeyed through the area of the Moqui Indians (Tusayan), López de Cárdenas got near the Grand Canyon and Melchor Díaz reached the mouth of the Colorado. The other members of the expedition wandered in the region of Cicuye (Pecos), Acoma, Tigüex, Taos and Jémez.

The conquest of New Mexico was begun by Juan de Oñate in the midst of hardship and attempts to find Cíbola and the Strait of Anián. In 1607 he gave up the attempt at conquest because of lack of success, and it was not until 1692 that Spanish authority was decisively established in these regions thanks to Diego de Vargas Zapata Luján and Ponce de León.

The search for the northern strait called Anián resulted in the discovery of the Californias and the constant organization of exploratory journeys to them. These were the fruits that the Spanish obtained from those dreams of the seven legendary cities and the strait of Anián.

Money, talent and men were wasted in the course of the 12 expeditions to the north, undertaken by the conquistadors between 1532 an 1602 that never fulfilled their purpose.

It was the Jesuits who succeeded in establishing a grand total of 18 missions in the north. Deserving mention is Father Juan de Ugarte who made the vow to stay in these regions although his colleague Father Salvatierra had already abandoned the missions that had been founded.

In the 18th century, the Spanish government decided to populate New California because it feared invasion at these points by the expanding nations of Russia and England.

To settle California, Spain made use of the Franciscans, who founded 21 missions with the help of Don José Galvez. The first of these was San Diego, established in 1769, followed by Monterrey the next year, and later all the others. A notable figure in this period when the north was being settled was Fray Junípero Serra.

The north of Mexico was the scene of great dreams and bold expeditions, but as a concrete result remained a group of scattered missions that were for a long time centers

*"the city of Tenochtitlan
fell into
the hands of Cortés..."*

of colonization and evangelization for the natives of the region.

It was largely as a result of the territory conquered in the north that the Kingdom of New Spain finally covered almost 4 million square kilometers.

Colonial Mexico

The Colony, in Mexico, is that long period of three centuries (16th, 17th and 18th) during which a population settled down, not without instances of violence, on the vast territory of New Spain.

During these centuries, Spanish authority extended over a population composed of Spaniards, who held the main posts in the government of New Spain, and natives, who, after much Christian philosophical reflection, were considered free. In the eyes of the law they were minors. They were organized into labor forces in 'Encomiendas' and later in 'Repartimientos', and payed tribute to the Spanish Crown which ceded its rights to the encomendero (holder of crown-granted lands). They were not subject to the jurisdiction of the Holy Office (Inquisition).

In addition to Spaniards and natives, the society of colonial Mexico included negroes who had been brought to New Spain as slaves to do the heavy work and so make up for the natives' lack of strength.

The children of Spaniards born in New Spain were called Creoles and made up another important social group with its own characteristics created by the environment.

In time, these races mixed and castes originated, the main ones being mestizos (Indian and Spanish blood); mulattos (Negro and Spanish blood), and zambos (Indian and Negro blood). It was these races and castes that made up the greater portion of the population of New Spain.

During these three centuries, the highest authority recognized in New Spain was the King, whether of the Austrian house or Bourbon. Because of the great distance, the kings could not govern their overseas possessions directly, and so created two organizations to administer their colonies. One, called the Casa de Contratación de Sevilla (1503) was concerned with looking after the economic interests of the Crown in the American possessions, the other, El Consejo de Indias (1524) directed administrative matters.

Three types of government followed one another in New Spain: the personal government of Cortés, the Audiencias and the Viceroyalty. The government of Cortés was approved by the Crown, and he ruled over the territories he had conquered with the title of Governor and Captain General for a short but beneficial and fertile period. He ordered the introduction of new crops and the establishment of cattle ranching, created sugar mills and made several important geographical explorations. He asked for and favored the first missionaries to arrive in Mexico.

However, Cortés made the serious mistake of leaving his captains in power to go to Las Hibueras (Honduras) to punish Cristóbal de Olid, who had disobeyed him with the idea of conquering the area on his own. Later, Cortés was tried for accusations made against him, but these were never proved and he was able to defend himself against them. After a life full of great efforts and glory, Cortés died in Castilleja de la Cuesta on December 2, 1547. His remains lie in the Hospital de Jesús in Mexico City.

After the government of Cortés and his deputies, the government of the 'Audiencias' was established. There were two of them, created to correct the damage that the previous governments had done to the Crown. The warrant signed by Charles V and dated Burgos, December 13, 1527 was the one that established the Audiencia in Mexico.

The Audiencia was a real court of justice, consisting of the President, eight jurists, four magistrates, two officers — one accusing and one defending — a constable and other less important members.

The First Audiencia began to function in December 1528, with Nuño de Beltrán de Guzmán as president and Alonso de Parada, Francisco Maldonado, Juan Ortiz de Matienzo and Diego Delgadillo as jurists. Shortly after their arrival in Mexico, Maldonado and Parra died, and were replaced by Gonzalo de Salazar. The government of the First Audiencia was disastrous and unjust.

Many complaints reached the Spanish Cortes about the priests and Bishop Zumárraga for the bad government of the First Audiencia, and these complaints were one of the reasons why the King named new jurists. The Bishop of Hispaniola, Sebastián Ramírez de Fuenteal, was named president, and Vasco de Quiroga, Alonso Maldonado, Francisco Zeinos and Juan de Salmerón were the jurists, all honest men who always governed justly, with the common good in sight. This Audiencia survived until 1535, when the Emperor, in a warrant dated Barcelona, April 17, 1535, ordered the creation of the Viceroyalty in New Spain.

The Viceroy, held wide powers, since he was governor, captain general, vicepatron, judge and superintendent of the royal estate (Hacienda). As governor, the Viceroy had to designate mayors (alcaldes mayores), provosts (corregidores) and certain temporary governors; supervised the health services and invigilated public morals of the settlers. As captain general, he was responsible for both internal and external defense of the kingdom. In his capacity as vicepatron, he interceded in the establishment of parishes and the organization of colleges and institutions of learning directed by the church. As judge, the Viceroy presided over the Audiencia, and as superintendant of the royal estate had a hand in the administration of public funds.

The principal duties of the Viceroy were to serve as a link between the people and the crown; defend these territories from foreign domination; make discoveries and conquests, and to ensure that the Indians were treated fairly and were converted to Christianity.

There were 62 Viceroys in all, who held their posts first for three years, then for five. The most outstanding of them were Don Antonio de Mendoza, the first Viceroy of Mexico; Don Luis de Velasco, father and son; Don Juan de Palafox y Mendoza, Fray Payo Enríquez de Rivera, Don Antonio María de Bucareli y Ursua, and the Second Count of Revillagigedo, Juan Vicente de Güemes Pacheco de Padilla.

In his government the Viceroy was helped by the Audiencias of Mexico City and Guadalajara, the Tribunal of the Holy Office or Inquisition, the 'Acordada' (rural police), the Corregidores (provosts) and others.

The economy of New Spain all through the colonial period was based on mining, agriculture, cattle ranching industry and commerce. Mining was the richest source of income for the first two centuries of the Viceroyalty, and the mines, although exploited privately were the property of the King. Agriculture was enriched constantly by new crops unknown in Mexico until this time, and ranching was a Spanish innovation, since cattle were unknown in pre-Cortesian Mexico. Various industries developed, such as handicrafts, silverworking, spinning and weaving, tanning and ironworking among others. New Spain carried on trade with the Iberian Peninsula, Cuba and the Philippines, and was another facet of economy cultivated by the Colony that helped to strengthen it.

Missionary activity was also important in the Viceroyalty. During the time Cortés was governor, Fray Pedro de Gante, Fray Juan de Ahora and Fray Juan de Tecto, all Franciscans, had arrived in Mexico. These, along with many others who arrived later, worked magnificently to civilize the country, teaching arts and occupations, building cities, aqueducts and roads, organizing villages and above all protecting the Indians.

During the colonial period, every monastery was a center of indoctrination and teaching, and the education of the native population is entirely due to the priests. We know that there were colleges for mestizos, for Indian nobles and ordinary native people, founded by Fray Juan de Zumárraga and Fray Pedro de Gante. In addition to these, the College of San Nicolás in Michoacán, founded by Don Vasco de Quiroga, the Real Seminario de Minería (the Royal School of Mining) and the Real Pontifica Universidad de México (Royal and Pontifical University of Mexico) were all temples of learning for those who wished to study at a higher level.

Mexico boasted of the first printing press on the Continent, thanks to the insistence of Fray Juan de Zumárraga, who had it brought. The first newspaper to circulate in the Viceroyalty was the 'Gaceta de México y Noticias de Nueva

España' (1722), and later appeared the 'Diario de México' and 'Pensador Mexicano'.

New Spain did not only encourage learning and journalism but also made names in art, history, literature and science. We shall list the most notable figures in these fields of learning.

In history, Francisco López de Gomarra, who wrote the 'Crónica de la Conquista de Nueva España' ('Chronicle of the Conquest of New Spain'), Cortés with his 'Cartas de Relación', Bernal Díaz del Castillo with 'La Verdadera historia de la conquista de la Nueva España' ('The True History of the Conquest of New Spain'). Fray Bartolomé de las Casas wrote, among other works, 'Historia de las Indias' ('History of the Indies'); Hernando Alvarado Tezozomoc, the 'Crónica Mexicana' ('Mexican Chronicle'); Fernando de Alva Ixtlilxochitl, the Historia Chichimeca ('History of the Chichimecs'). Fray Juan de Torquemada, 'Monarquía Indiana' ('American Indian Monarchy'), and Francisco Javier Clavijero wrote the 'Historia Antigua de México' ('Ancient History of Mexico'). In addition to those mentioned in the field of history, there are others who linked dates and events to give us a picture of ancient and colonial Mexico.

In poetry, the outstanding figures are Gutierre de Cetina and Fray Miguel de Guevara. Juan Ruiz de Alarcón was a famous playwright, Carlos de Sigüenza y Góngora a noted scientist and man of letters; Juana de Asbaje, known as Sor Juana Inés de la Cruz (1651-1695) gained a reputation in literature.

Science, history and literature formed a well defined cultural world through the colonial period.

Art and architecture are also part of the marvelous cultural world that vibrated during the three centuries of

*"every monastery
was a center of indoctrination
and teaching. . ."*

the Colony. Various styles of architecture existed, all of them beautiful. The Moorish style, exemplified by the Capilla Real at Cholula that gives the impression of a mosque, Franciscan Gothic has Plateresque (Renaissance) features and the constructions are solid, having very high walls topped with purely decorative merlons, and ogival rose windows. This style, typical of the first half of the 16th century, was introduced by the Franciscans who used in their churches and convents mainly in the states of Tlaxcala, Hidalgo and Oaxaca. Examples of it can be found at Tula, Cuernavaca, Tlaxcala, Cholula and Huejotzingo. The Augustinians also constructed in this style at Actopan, Atotonilco el Grande, Yuriria, Acolman and Mérida cathedral where the buildings have Plateresque elements.

The 'Herreriano' style is characterized by its severity within classical Greco-roman lines; it is massive, stark, and makes no use of light and shade. This style, introduced by Juan de Herrera, is exemplified by Puebla cathedral.

The Baroque style exists in two forms, the Bernini and Borronini. The first one of them preserves Italian Renaissance lines and admits florid decoration and unnecessary elements. Examples of this style are the churches of Jesús María, San Lorenzo and San Hipólito in Mexico City. The Borronini form is developed at the discretion of the architect since he himself creates the proportions and ornamentation. This style can be found at the colleges of San Idelfonso and that of San Ignacio de las Vizcaínas in the capital. Other notable Baroque buildings are the Capilla del Rosario (Rosary Chapel) in Puebla, the church of La Profesa in Mexico City and Morelia cathedral.

Mexican Churrigueresque is made up of Baroque structures inclining to the Plateresque and profuse Gothic decoration. It is a style that expresses the burning faith and at the same time the great wealth of New Spain in the 18th century. Constructions in this style are the Sagrario, the church of La Santísima and the lateral doorway of the church of San Francisco, all in Mexico City. Elsewhere are the Colegio de los Jesuitas (Jesuit College) at Tepotzotlán, the Church of La Valenciana in Guanajuato, and the convents of San Agustín, Santa Rosa and Santa Clara in Querétaro.

The Academic or Neoclassical style was born to counteract the Churrigueresque and was established in Mexico by Manuel Tolsá and Francisco Tresguerras. The former built the Colegio de Minería (Mining School) and the Casa de Pinillos in Mexico City. Tresguerras was responsible for the Casa Rul in Guanajuato and in Celaya for the altars, portico and dome of the churches of El Carmen and San Francisco. He also built the Ruiz de Alarcón theater and the independence monument in San Luis Potosí.

The painting of the Viceroyalty went through several stages. In the 16th century we see murals painted *a fresco* using only three colors: black, red and yellow, and small pictures on altarpieces. In the 17th century appear the large oil paintings showing great realism, sober colors, balanced chiaroscuro and exactness of line. Belonging to the 18th century are great canvases in oils that however lack originality and observation, being simply repetitions of conventional subjects or landscapes.

The outstanding artists of the time, among others are Andrés de la Concha, Baltazar de Echave Orio, Cristóbal de Villalpando, Miguel Cabrera and Juan Correa. They enriched the world of painting with their oils, some secular, but most of them dealing with religious themes, all showing a master's touch.

The colonial period was affected by political events in the Iberian peninsula. It was at this moment that the desire for independence flowered in Mexico and a long series of important events began that form the history of Independent Mexico.

The Independence

Some authors say that during the colonial period Mexico enjoyed a long era of calm and unshakable peace. According to this view of history, life in New Spain went on placidly until 1810, when a long series of social and political struggles began that profoundly affected the harmony that had reigned in the country through three centuries of Spanish rule.

However, from the beginning, social, economic and political antagonism had existed, that originated in the unequal distribution of wealth and in the political and legal privileges enjoyed by the ruling groups. Throughout the colonial period there were constant uprisings of Indians, Negros and Castes, but there were also rebellions by Spaniards and insurrections and plots on the part of Creoles and euromestizos.

In addition to the rebel movement that grew up mainly for economic and social reasons, New Spain was also shaken by the continual conflicts between the clergy and the representatives of the State, and between the ecclesiastical institutions themselves. Most of the insurrections that occurred during the colonial period were fundamentally class struggles, and these created a revolutionary spirit long before the emancipation movement of 1810.

The independence of Mexico was also influenced by external developments which were, in chronological order, European thought, particularly the ideas of the Enlightenment and the French Encyclopedists; the industrial revolution in Britain that began around 1760 and the expansion of British power in America; the independence of the United States and its commercial and territorial expansion; the French Revolution, begun in 1789 and its political principles; Napoleon's invasion of Spain. Ideas, political events, revolutions, interests of other nations were all external factors that fused with Mexico's aspirations towards political liberty and the social and economic interests to produce the revolution.

In spite of this, it must be realized that the independence of Mexico was due to direct internal causes, rather than influence from outside. The social injustice that prevailed in New Spain, where peninsular Spaniards and the Creoles enjoyed privileges, posts and wealth to the detriment of the lower classes, had already produced in the last decades of the 18th century separatist movements, that had apparently been suppressed. There was also discontent about the monopolies and state stores, and about the prohibition on the manufacture of specific articles and the cultivation of certain crops in order to favor Spanish trade. The result of all this was that the peninsular Spaniards and the Creoles, who were not content to obey without argument, inclined in favor of a separation from Spain, that would allow the colony to enjoy its riches, using them for its own profit and creating new sources of prosperity.

The abdication of Charles IV in favor of Napoleon on May 8, 1808, and the invasion of Spain by French armies created among the Spanish elements in the colony a unique situation that strengthened the ideas of autonomy. The French occupation produced an economic crisis in which the Spanish people waged a war of liberation and created juntas to direct the uprising. These were dominated by members with a liberal ideology, advocates of sovereignty of the people, constitutional monarchy, division of power, equality of rights between Spaniards and Americans, etc.

Events in Spain immediately caused serious repercussions in New Spain that finally led to armed rebellion. Neither the authorities appointed by the King, nor the Spaniards and Creoles could reach agreement on the way to govern the colony while Spain was fighting the French.

When the struggle against intervention broke out in the Iberian Peninsula, the Viceroy of New Spain, José Iturriaga supported by the Creole faction that was in favor of the idea of autonomy in a way proclaimed the provisional independence of Mexico. The Spaniards overthrew him and put New Spain under the authority of the Central Junta that was governing Spain. The Creoles could not forgive this; they were almost unanimous in thinking that they were dependent on Charles IV, not on the Spanish people, a new entity, legally unconnected with the conquest and the governing of the colony. They waited, plotted, felt that they had reached maturity, were aware that they formed an authentic society and convinced that they could liberate themselves.

Plots were hatched in various cities such as Morelia (Valladolid), but the most important conspiracy was made in Querétaro where there was a sizeable group of organizers including the Corregidor of the town Miguel Domínguez and his wife, Josefa Ortiz de Domínguez, Captain Ignacio Allende and the priest of the village of Dolores, Miguel Hidalgo y Costilla. By September 1810, the conspiracy had spread to various settlements and haciendas in the Bajío thanks to the work of the revolutionary, Allende.

Patriotic feelings were summarized in the phrase: "New Spain for the Americans", but to achieve this it was necessary to snatch it from the Spaniards. Allende realized this perfectly well and for this reason entrusted the command of the movement to Hidalgo who had tremedous prestige among the population due to his position as priest, although his notion of independence was social because it meant the emancipation of the Indians.

The revolution was due to break out in December 1810 during a great trade fair that was held in one of the Bajío cities, but the plan was discovered and the conspirators, rallying round Hidalgo, decided to proclaim the insurrection in the early morning of September 16. They left the town of Dolores with 600 men, but in a few days brought the number up to 1,000. Rather than an army, these looked like a crowd of demonstrators armed with sticks and slings.

They took possession of San Miguel, Celaya and Salamanca without resistance. Guanajuato, an important mining city, fell after a bloody struggle and was sacked. Later this 'army' took the city of Valladolid (Morelia) and from there set out towards the almost unprotected Mexico City. They won the battle of Monte de las Cruces on the outskirts of the city, and began their withdrawal, during which they were defeated at San Jerónimo Aculco by the Spanish general, Félix María Calleja.

In fact, none of the revolutionary leaders had time to organize a plan. Hidalgo struggled to keep his control over the undisciplined masses that followed him to the cry of "Long live Our Lady of Guadalupe and Death to the bad

Government", but for them, liberty was not a right, not a natural way of thinking but an explosion of both hate and joy. Allende was determined to create a military nucleus in order to withdraw from this wild army later, but the job was impossible. Hidalgo was successful by humoring the mob, a course of action which had tragic results such as the massacres of Spaniards in Guanajuato, Valladolid (Morelia) and Guadalajara, that put up an unsurmountable barrier between the revolutionaries, who were called insurgents, and the Spaniards, or royalists. In this way, any negotiation became impossible.

Although Hidalgo had no definite program of reform, he did attempt to put into practice some measures that demonstrate the social character of his idea of independence. His orders refer to contemporary questions of the movement, such as the promise to give land to the Indians and castes, that was to attract great numbers of the native population. On December 5, 1810 he decreed the handing over of agricultural land to the natives, and the exclusive right to the use of their communal lands. Later, on the 15th of the same month, he abolished by a decree, slavery and the tributes that weighed heavily on the Indians and mestizos. Thus, Hidalgo introduced agrarian elements into the struggle for independence.

In 1811, faced by the sight of a revolution that threatened to change social structure and the system of property in operation, the Creoles in favor of the revolution began to join the defenders of the colonial regime. Although Hidalgo tried to convince them that the struggle was against the Spaniards and not against them, the Creoles noticed that the fight for emancipation was also a war of castes.

Just as Hidalgo stood for the civil element, Allende represented the military and Creole elements, and this was the origin of disagreements and conflicts. For the Creoles, independence meant simply a separation from Spain and the substitution of local elements for Spanish ones in the government of the colony; for the Indians and the castes, the movement was social and directed against exploiters, either Spanish or Creole. Allende himself saw the revolution only as an exercise that had to be carried out by strict military means, something not possible because of the lack of arms and the makeshift nature of the crowd that he and Hidalgo were leading. In time this difference of opinions gradually divided the revolutionary group.

After defeat at Aculco, Hidalgo made for Guadalajara where he organized an army of 30 thousand men, with which he confronted Calleja at Puente de Calderón. The revolutionary forces lost the battle, and the survivors fled towards Zacatecas but, pursued by the royalists continued northward where they fell into a trap laid by a former insurgent, Ignacio Elizondo. Hidalgo and his companions were taken prisoner in Chihuahua and shot in the middle of the year 1811.

Be that as it may, the movement had spread. Groups were rising to arms everywhere; partisans of the new ideas, soldiers, lawyers or clerics sympathetic to the people's feeling of social injustice, headed sporadic rebellions. While one part of the Mexican population was fighting the Viceregal government, another accepted the Spanish government's invitation to attend the Congress of Cadiz and take part in the drawing up of the Spanish Liberal Constitution of 1812.

On Hidalgo's death, the banner of the insurgents was raised again by José María Morelos y Pavón, parish priest of Carácuaro, Michoacán and Ignacio López Rayón, a comrade of the first insurgents.

Opposite López Rayón, an educated Creole afraid of a popular revolution, stood Morelos as the representative

"Allende. . . entrusted the command of the movement to Hidalgo who had tremendous prestige. . ."

of the exploited classes and the interpreter of the real purposes of the movement of rebellion. López Rayón tried to organize the insurgents, creating a junta that was to keep New Spain for Ferdinand VII, the Zitácuaro Junta. Morelos did not agree with continuing to talk about the rights of the Spanish monarch but rather about the rights of New Spain, and for this reason forced the drawing up of the first Mexican Constitution.

Between 1811 and 1814, the military action of the insurgents was more important than their political activity. From the very beginning Morelos understood it was necessary to substitute Hidalgo's indisciplined rabble with small but disciplined and above all adequately equipped armies. His army never rose above 6 thousand, and with it he carried out the most brilliant campaigns of the liberation movement, using guerrilla fighting as an auxiliary method.

Later he put all his efforts into the task of organizing the political and legal aspects of the revolution for independence, summoning and protecting a Congress that was to draw up a Constitution. Morelos thus emerges as both a military genius and a political and social reformer.

In 1813, after his brilliant campaigns in Cuautla, Oaxaca and Acapulco, Morelos summoned a congress in Chilpancingo with the idea of bringing in line the tendencies of the insurgent movement and of replacing the Zitácuaro Junta, a political body weakened and discredited by disagreement among its members. It was imperative to ensure the insurgents' unity of action through a strong central government.

On September 14, 1813 Morelos read before this Congress his historic document known as "Sentimientos de la Nación" ("Feelings of the Nation"), in which he defined his political and social convictions at the same time as he made clear the ambitions of the people: separation from Spain and any other government or monarchy, sovereignty of the people, division of powers, legal equality, work only for Americans, governmental reforms, expulsion of the Spaniards, freedom of trade, respect for property, the abolition of torture, the disappearance of tributes and monopolies and the abolition of castes and slavery. The Congress of Chilpancingo sat for four months, and on November 16, proclaimed the Act of Independence.

The leader's long pause for political activities allowed the royalist army under Calleja to be reorganized. Morelos was defeated at Valladolid, and the Congress had to keep on the move until at Apatzingán, on October 22, 1814, it issued the first Mexican Constitution.

However, this was inspired more by the 1973 French Constitution and the 1812 Spanish Constitution than by the social and political principles of Morelos. Apart from doing nothing to moderate the immense wealth of the rich and alleviate the misery of the poor, it deposited executive power in the hands of the three people, not one, opening the door to anarchy within the revolutionary movement that was so in need of leadership at that time. The authors of the Constitution, inspired by romantic and liberal ideas that reflected the doctrines of the bourgeois revolution in Europe, wished to establish a centralized republican government and worked as representatives of the interests of the landowners and clergy of New Spain.

The Constitution of Apatzingán could not be put into practice, because when it was declared the insurgents had already been chased out of the south. At the end of 1815 when the Congress was trying to establish itself at Tehuacán under the protection of Morelos, the leader was defeated, taken prisoner, and shot at San Cristóbal Ecatepec on December 22.

With the death of Morelos the period of decline of the insurgents movement began. The years from 1816 to 1819 are characterized by defensive fighting in which guerrilla warfare played the most important part. Only the military campaigns of Vicente Guerrero in the south, and the meteoric career of the Spanish liberal, Francisco Javier Mina can be considered as military movements in which defense was not the salient feature.

The Congress of Chilpancingo was dissolved by a rebel leader, the first coup d'état in the history of the embryo republic, and even though some 30 thousand men were calculated to be still fighting for independence, by this time their hold on the important regions was shortlived. The most important rebel nuclei in those years were Vicente Guerrero's in the south, that of Guadalupe Victoria and Nicolás Bravo in the Veracruz area, Osorno's around Puebla and Hidalgo, and Ramón Rayón's in Michoacán. Bands of guerrillas, consisting of patriots but also of men greedy for plunder, devastated the roads and made themselves hated by the villages. There was no discipline among these fighters, but there were ambitions and disputes over leadership.

If this was happening in the rebel camp, the outrages committed by the royalists were no less. Supported by the policy of repression of Calleja, named Viceroy of New Spain, some royalist leaders held up the convoys they were supposed to protect to take possession of the merchandise and resell it later. One of these leaders who distinguished himself in particular was Agustín de Iturbide.

In the course of the third period of the war of insurgents, especially from 1818 on, a very important change began to make itself felt in the colony. Creoles and Spaniards started to discuss more seriously the advantages that would result from an independent government. They were aware that capital was lacking because of the wars of Spain, that the scarcity and high prices of commodities were a result of a policy that prevented free trade, and that concessions were granted freely in the Peninsula but not in New Spain.

Creole leaders and officers predominated in the royalist army by whose efforts the Viceroy's government was able to carry out repressive action against the rebellion, but the ideas of liberty and independence began to influence these men also, thanks to the Scottish freemasons who had settled in the country a few years before. In addition, the obstinate resistance of Guerrero and other insurgents invited new political action, this time in order to achieve independence from Spain. This new set of circumstances caused a political change of direction that was climaxed by the liberation of Mexico.

After a decade of revolution, independence had become the cause not only of the rebels, but also of the privileged classes, and it was the reinstatement of the constitutional monarchy in Spain in 1820, with the resulting reestablishment of the Constitution of Cadiz in 1812, that made them ready to fight for autonomy.

In this year (1820) a liberal-inspired uprising forced Ferdinand VII, Charles IV's successor, to put into effect again the liberal reforms of 1812. The Spanish Cortes, composed of zealous liberals, prepared measures against the property and immunity of the clergy. The news of these changes caused profound discontent among the Spaniards and the Creole aristocracy of Mexico.

With its privileges and property threatened, the Church in New Spain radically opposed the constitutional government that had triumphed in the Peninsula and had been gaining a foothold in New Spain.

The great landowners, rich merchants, high ranks in the army and even the Creole officials who considered themselves held back from promotion by the Spaniards in Mexico, coincided with the clergy in a rebellious attitude. Now independence was going to be accomplished, on the understanding that the interests and privileges of the Spaniards who allied themselves with the Creoles in this undertaking would remain protected.

It was Matías Monteagudo, agent of the high clergy of New Spain that organized and directed the conspiracy of La Profesa whose members, impatient to bring about the separation from Spain to save property and privileges, elected Agustín de Iturbide to head a military rising in the service of the high clergy and the Creole and Spanish aristocracy.

Supported by the conspirators, Iturbide obtained the command of an army assigned to fight and destroy Guerrero, but having failed he decided to bring about independence with the participation of the rebel leader. Iturbide made a pact with Guerrero, and this alliance produced the Iguala Plan, proclaimed on February 24, 1821, also known as the Plan of the Three Guarantees. This established a single religion, a union of all the social groups and the independence of Mexico, with the adoption of the system of constitutional monarchy until the arrival of a European king.

The Iguala movement quickly spread over the whole country, thanks to Iturbide's double campaign — military and diplomatic — in five months. Without the support of the Creoles, for 10 years the staunchest supporters of the colonial regime, independence was an established fact. The military campaign was short and bloodless, because many leaders and officers, both Creole and Spanish decided to support the Iguala Plan together with the forces they commanded.

On August 24, 1821, in the town of Córdoba, Juan O'Donjú, the last Spanish Viceroy, and Agustín de Iturbide, representing the Mexican Empire, signed the Treaty of Córdoba, which confirmed in essence the plan of the Three Guarantees. On September 27 the army led by Iturbide made its triumphal entry into Mexico City.

In the struggle for independence, the Spaniards won over the Creoles and these in their turn, the insurgents. United in a common aim, they were to separate at the very moment it was achieved, because the insurgents could not give up their fight until their ideas were put fully into effect. Mexican independence had been achieved by the union of Spaniards and Americans and by the establishment of a monarchy that left the economic, political and social structure of New Spain intact.

The First Empire

On achieving an independent life, Mexico found itself without the social elements necessary to make a true nation. The inhabitants had been used to "keeping silent and obeying" for three centuries of Spanish rule, and now had to find their way to autonomy through a period of anarchy and fighting, searching for a pattern on which to base their new status.

At the moment of independence, society was dominated by a powerful clergy that in 300 years had succeeded in accumulating in its hands the greater part of the property of the nation, and in addition, made use of the influence it had over the population through teaching, the pulpit and the confessional to spread the principles and ideas that could strengthen its authority. On the other hand the war of independence had created a military class that had not existed before. From 1821 it obtained promotions and privileges that allowed it to influence the life of the country decisively through uprisings — its favorite occupation—almost always as the strong arm of the church.

Every element of order was destroyed by the permanent state of civil war that seemed to be leading the country inevitably to ruin. In a brief period of 33 years, from 1821 to 1854, there was an empire, five Constitutions were drawn up, two federal and two centralized political systems were established, two foreign wars were fought, in the second of which the country lost half its territory, and in the last years of this period, Antonio López de Santa Anna, with the support of the conservatives, set up a dictatorship.

Mexico, then, was looking for a pattern on which to organize itself. Some claimed to find it in the past, maintaining the institutions of the colonial régime, others thought it lay in the future through the transformation of the political system and society.

The inevitable result of all these conflicting tendencies was a chronic state of social and political dispute that lasted until the privileges, customs and institutions derived from the colonial system disappeared.

With independence won, social and economic reform remained to be carried out, a much more difficult task than simple political liberation. To accomplish this, capable men determined to fight all obstacles without yielding to the interests of individuals or bodies were indispensable. At the beginning there were some, but they did not achieve anything because their actions lacked firmness and their demands clarity and because they were working in conditions unfavorable to their aims. When this difficult stage was over, new men appeared who put into operation a clear and precise program of social reform.

Some authors call the period from 1821 to 1854 the era of Santa Anna, which could not be more exact. For more than a quarter of a century Santa Anna was the strong man of Mexico, and his name was pronounced in all the rebellions. A past master of political intrigue, he served all parties, and transformed parties and men into instruments of his own ambition; an opportunist of genius, he always knew the exact moment when to back the party that had strength and power. However, to blame him for all that happened during these years, for all the disturbances and upheavals of the period is to confuse one of the principal authors of the drama through which Mexico was slowly and painfully developing its national identity, with the drama itself.

When Mexico became independent from Spain, it adopted the system of government by constitutional monarchy with the executive power represented by a provisional Regency, until such time as Ferdinand VII or one of the Bourbon princes should come to occupy the throne of Mexico. A Council of Worthies was formed, with the name of Junta Provisional Gubernativa (Provisional Governing Council) which was given legislative powers, while a Congress was convened whose job it was to draw up the Constitution of the Mexican Empire.

The Council of Worthies was composed of representatives of the high clergy, the royalist party, and those who had played important parts in the triumph of the Iguala Plan. In September 1821, this body designated the members of the Regency, naming Iturbide as president and also giving him the post of generalissimo. In this way, Iturbide consolidated his position as head of the Creole military party whose ambition was to govern the country permanently.

The Constitutional Congress was convened and began sessions on February 24 the following year. The majority of the deputies were Creoles full of the ideas of the French and North American revolutions and sympathizers of the republican system. There were few monarchists, divided into two groups, one supporting the Bourbons that wanted Ferdinand or a Bourbon prince as king, and one in favor of crowning Iturbide.

Shortly after the Congress began sessions, the news reached Mexico that the Spanish Cortes did not ratify the Treaty of Córdoba, considering it illegal and invalid. So, the only article left standing was the one establishing the right to the Mexican throne of the person that the Cortes of Mexico named, with the result that the monarchist party rallied round Iturbide.

The progress of events now gathered speed. The Congress delegates were still discussing the political constitution they were trying to give to Mexico when, on the night of May 18, 1822, an infantry sergeant called Pío Marcha, and the colonel of grenadiers, Epitacio Sánchez, certainly instruments of the Iturbide faction, incited the soldiers of the city garrison to declare themselves for the author of the Iguala Plan. The following day the Congress, under pressure from public opinion, elected Iturbide emperor with the title of Agustín I.

The creation of an empire was a political necessity in the face of the arrogance of the Royal House of Spain that refused to recognize its former colony's right to an independent government. It was mainly by the support of the Creole soldiers that Iturbide became emperor. The clergy the privileged classes, the majority of the army and the common people were for him. The Spaniards, some of the former insurgents and the republicans declared themselves against him.

The Empire, in spite of its popularity, was stillborn because it was destitute from the beginning and because it disappointed so many who saw in it a "philosopher's stone", a sort of formula to change the natural wealth of the country into gold. On the other hand, news about Bourbon or republican and insurgent conspiracies helped to increase the uneasiness of Mexican society, and aroused the fear of new rebellions.

From the start the disagreements between Iturbide and the Congress were evident. The emperor, violating the constitutional privilege of the delegates, had the most prominent ones arrested simply because they were his enemies. The Congress, for its part, had lived by politics; unpracticed in administration, and faced with the necessity of maintaining an army of 35 thousand men ready for war, it let the treasury live on existing funds, which increased the financial deficit with which Mexico began its life of independence. The conflict finally came to a head when Iturbide chose the wrong moment to propose an electoral reform that tended to reduce the number of delegates by half.

The proposal was rejected, and because of Congress' hostility towards him, Iturbide dissolved it on October 31, 1882. In its place he named a Junta Instituyente that took up its position on November 2 of the same year.

In general, the situation of the country could not have been more discouraging. The Spanish forces still occupying the castle of San Juan de Ulúa off the coast of Veracruz hindered the movement of trade in the port; the provinces, under the excuse of liberty, were the scene of anarchy; the Central American countries, at first joined to the Empire, were trying to form independent states. The treasury was empty, and while a loan was being negotiated under the severest conditions, the Junta Instituyente, to meet the most pressing demands of the moment, resorted to imposing heavy taxes and to antieconomic measures such as prohibiting the export of money and creating paper money that it was obligatory to use. While expenses had risen, earnings were diminishing because of lack of confidence in the stability of the government; industry was paralysed, the mines were hardly producing, and agriculture and trade, after 11 years of war for independence, were ruined.

It was Antonio López de Santa Anna who began the revolt against the Empire when he rose up in Veracruz on December 6, 1822 proclaiming the Republic. Creole soldier and former royalist leader, Santa Anna won over to his cause the provincial government of Veracruz, the Spanish merchants and three former insurgents, Nicolás Bravo, Vicente Guerrero and Guadalupe Victoria. In January of the following year, general Antonio Echávarri, sent by Iturbide to fight Santa Anna, joined the enemy.

Agustín de Iturbide, in an attempt to control the situation, recalled the Congress he had previously dissolved and shortly afterwards, having no means to oppose the rebellion, submitted his abdication to the assembly. In March 1823 he went into exile and his public life came to an end.

Republican Rule

The Congress, reinstated under pressure of a revolution, rejected the abdication of Iturbide and declared that the Empire had been illegitimate from the beginning, which was not true. Also in order to quash all hopes of a restoration of the monarchy, it declared the Iguala Plan null and void in its references to the Bourbon princes. This act gave rise to two legally formed parties, the Mexican imperialist and the Hispanoamerican, or Bourbonist, and one indisputable fact: the Republic.

The problem then was, what sort of republic. The most cultured part of the triumphant oligarchy, the high clergy, the principal members of the army and the landowners were in favor of a republic on the lines of France, in which the capital would be predominant and the provinces subordinate to it, which was derived from the viceregal system and which was probably the most sensible at that moment. Part of the Congress was inclined to agree with this point of view; the Bourbonist party joined this group that began to call itself centralist and in which there were important politicians such as Lucas Alamán, Fray Servando Teresa de Mier and Miguel Santa María. All the conservatives of the country supported them, including the section that commanded almost all the trade and a large part of the mining activities and agriculture, the Spaniards.

A curious political phenomenon was the result. The reform party, that began to distinguish itself by its disagreement with the Spaniards and the privileged groups who it considered to be the main obstacle to its aims, instead of being centralist as in France, was federalist and proposed a republic on the pattern of North America, whose constitution it had studied. Miguel Ramos Arizpe, Lorenzo de Zavala, Valentín Gómez Farías and others tried to organize this party and could count on a powerful aid "Iturbidism", that was stirring up the feeling of localism in all parts of the country.

The political tendencies of the parties being formed were shown through the masonic lodges that during these years became veritable political parties in which the representatives of the various groups took part and acted. In turn the lodges, became divided into Scottish and Yorkist. To the first kind belonged the conservatives or centralists, that is to say clerics, army leaders and great landowners; to the second, the representatives of the popular front and the federalists or liberals.

The Congress that had created the Empire realized that it was impossible for it to survive and after a few urgent measures of a financial and military nature, reduced its role to the job of convening a new Constitutional Congress and retired. In the new Congress the federalist elements were so important and numerous that the assembly considered itself called to legalize the Federation, which actually already existed in an anarchical form. On October 4, 1824 the Federal Constitution of the United States of Mexico was proclaimed, and on the 19th of the same month, Guadalupe Victoria was elected president of the new republic.

However, the brand-new political and social statute of the country did not make a complete break with the past; it upheld religious intolerance, ecclesiastical and military privileges were kept and the individual's rights against the power of the State were not established. Three million illiterate and poverty-stricken Indians, an inheritance from colonial rule were suddenly brought within civil law, acquiring theoretical equality with the other sections of the population. The Indian became a citizen, and even though the oppressive tributes were eliminated, as a citizen he now had to pay taxes and do military service, while the advantages and rights granted to him by the Constitution only existed on paper, as he lacked the ability to enjoy them.

At the end of Guadalupe Victoria's presidency, during which Mexican independence was finally recognized by the United States and England, a former insurgent, Vicente Guerrero became president in 1829 and in 1830 a military leader, Anastasio Bustamante. Guerrero was deposed by a Congress dominated by the Scottish and Yorkists, on which Bustamante, who had a supporting majority among the delegates, became president. Guerrero, not content with this decision, retired to Acapulco from where he continued to fight his successor, but he was captured by his enemies and shot at Cuilapa on February 14, 1831.

Bustamante's administration relied on the alliance of the army and the clergy. With the help of a young conservative, Lucas Alamán, Bustamante was determined to discipline the army, reorganize public finance, and seek reconciliation with Spain and the Vatican to obtain recognition of national independence. But civil war broke out again and both in the capital and the states a campaign grew up against the federal government, headed by Valentín Gómez Farías, head of a group of progressive politicians dedicated to overthrowing Bustamante to be able to carry out important political reforms.

At the beginning of 1832 the garrison of Veracruz rose against Bustamante, and Santa Anna again put himself at the head of a movement that quickly spread throughout the country. The president, unable to resist, had to resign.

In April 1833, the educated middle class, grouped around Gómez Farías and inspired by another liberal, José María Luis Mora, took the government of the country in its hands and placed Santa Anna in the presidency. The middle class, with the help of the civil militia, and an advanced liberal program, was going to attempt a reform that the country was not yet ready for, and which had the appearance of a complete social and political change.

The reformers of 1833 directed their actions against the economic and spiritual power of the church. With Gómez Farías as vicepresident, and Santa Anna retired on his hacienda, Manga de Clavo, the Government began to control ecclesiastical appointments and imposed penalties on the priests and bishop who did not obey the orders of the Federation. The Dirección de Instrucción Pública (Board of Public Education) was created, and it was decreed that teaching should be free and secular; the privileges of the clergy and the army were suppressed; Church property was seized; the separation of Church and State was established, and the State would now take over the registering of population and legalizing marriages, births, etc.

Both the army and the clergy declared war on the reformist decrees. The army because it saw itself deprived of its immunities and privileges that had in fact made it political arbiter of the country, and the Church because the new legislation deprived it suddenly of considerable revenues and, above all, took away the enormous power it held through religious teaching.

Various rebellions ruined the plans of the liberal reformers. Santa Anna himself, now defender of those he had fought, rose against his own vicepresident and repealed his laws in April 1834. A new Congress, assembled the following year, introduced the centralistic system.

The reform of the liberal middle class had been shortlived. Unable because of their origin and political and social principles to obtain the support of the poor, they managed to keep in power for only a short time. Their defeat permitted the establishment of a centralistic form of government, and the most important consequence of this was the declaration of the independence of Texas.

For long before 1821 the political unity of Mexican territory had been threatened by the expansionist tendencies of the United States. Shortly before Independence, the government of New Spain authorized the North American, Moses Austin to colonize the territory of Texas with any respectable Catholic families who acknowledged the authority of the King of Spain and observed the Liberal Constitution of 1812. When Mexico became independent the Texan settlers became subject to the authorities and laws of the new nation, which ratified the concession to colonize the territory in favor of Austin's son, Stephen.

The population of Texas was almost entirely Anglo-Saxon in origin and with more cultural ties with the United States than with Mexico. For this reason, when Anastasio

Bustamante issued a decree forbidding more foreign families to settle in Texas, the settlers felt that their interests were being affected. They had already made several attempts to break away from Mexico, but it was not until 1835 that they declared themselves independent, claiming that the Mexican nation had violated federative principals by adopting a centralistic system. Armed by the North Americans and with San Antonio in their power, the Texans faced the situation and waited for the Mexican armies to arrive.

At this point president Santa Anna personally led an army of 6 thousand to fight a war that most Mexicans felt was national. However, the Texas campaign not only showed up the breakaway state's inability to resist the Mexican army with its own resources, but also made very clear the political and military ineptitude of the general, of mutiny and of civil war.

At the beginning of 1836, Santa Anna triumphed in a part of Mexican territory between the Bravo (Grande) and Sabinas rivers. His policy was to harry the Texans by shooting prisoners, laying fields waste and burning villages. He defeated the Texan forces at San Antonio Béjar, El Alamo, San Patricia, Santa Rosa and El Perdido, but his policy caused the North Americans to side with the Texans and his strategy finally endangered his victorious advance in a rash adventure that led to the disaster of San Jacinto; there, the column he commanded was destroyed, and Santa Anna taken prisoner. The fear of losing his life made him convert partial defeat into a general disaster when he ordered the column led by Vicente Filisola to cross the Bravo and leave the state of Texas.

The military question was in fact now answered, because a new attempt to win back Texan territory would bring Mexico into a confrontation with the United States. On May

14, 1836, through the Velasco Treaty, the conflict was brought to an end. Mexico did not recognize Texan independence, but agreed to evacuate its troops from the area. As for Santa Anna, he accepted Texan independence and the drawing of frontiers beyond the Río Bravo in exchange for his freedom.

In spite of his conduct, Santa Anna was not tried, and the Congress did not ask for explanations. Ironically, at the moment when the result of the Texas campaign was learnt, and while measures were being taken to neutralize the effects of the defeat, the members were drawing up a new political code.

On December 30, 1836 the Constitution of the Seven Laws was published that reinforced the centralistic system. The following year, in the elections carried out in accordance with the new Constitution, Anastasio Bustamante was elected president.

This government was faced with not only the consequences of the Texan war, but also, in the three years from 1837 to 1839, a war with France and a separatist movement in Yucatán that was called the "War of the Castes".

In 1838 the French government sent a naval force to Mexico that took Veracruz, to obtain the satisfaction of claims for damages suffered by a French pastryshop in the capital during the national revolts. This war was given the name of the "Pastry War" and during the short time it lasted Santa Anna, called on by the federal government to lead the Mexican forces, lost his left foot. After a defeat at Veracruz, Mexico was in no condition to wage another war and saw itself obliged to sign a peace, on March 9, 1839, agreeing to pay 600,000 pesos indemnification.

The government's powerlessness to organize anything to subdue Yucatán, to field an army capable of imposing a

*"the North American forces
crossed
the Río Bravo..."*

definitive pact of mutal respect on the USA or make itself obeyed in the Departamentos was confirmed in 1841. Its constant need of finances led it to increase import tariffs and the businessmen brought about its fall.

Agents of import firms were constantly on the move between Veracruz and Guadalajara, via Mexico City. The prudent talked to the government about demonstrations; the determined showed themselves to be partisans of the great national panacea, revolution, uprising, what was popularly called "la bola" - "a shindy". And so, in August and September 1814 a military rebellion toppled the government of Bustamante. Generals Mariano Paredes Arrillaga, Gabriel Valencia and Santa Anna, the leaders, drew up the so-called Bases de Tacubaya, ignoring all powers except judicial, stipulating that two members should be elected by each Departamento to form a Congress, and Santa Anna was provisionally elected president. In actual fact, the Bases de Tacubaya established the dictatorship of Santa Anna.

This period of government by Santa Anna that lasted from 1841 to 1844 was characterized by the bad management of public finance, profusion of military posts, the sale of national property, the violation of laws and despotic military rule over all classes of society, including the clergy Tyranny finally produced an armed rising led by one of the generals who had supported the Bases de Tacubaya, Paredes Arrillaga, culminating in Santa Ann's exile, decreed by the Congress on May 27, 1845.

On the exile of the leader, General José Joaquín Herrera became president, and then the Congress turned its attention to the North American question that was now pressing.

After the separation of Texas in 1836, Mexico repeatedly declared that it still had legitimate rights in the occupied territory. The United States on their part, interested in annexing Texas definitively, encouraged raids by wild Indians in the frontier regions and even backed North American invasions with the obvious aim of creating motives for war with Mexico and obtaining territory to satisfy the ambitions of pro-slavery politicians.

Mexico however lacked the necessary financial resources to organize and lead northward an army to impose allegiance to the Mexican federation on Texas again. The fact was that the nation was almost brankrupt, there was no system of public finance, all the sources of wealth continued in a lamentable state of decadence and the common people, victims of economic backwardness and the treasury deficit were becoming more poverty stricken while they could see a fabulously rich Church and military leaders who seized the national funds as booty after every new revolt.

Meanwhile, Santa Anna, on assuming power in 1841, cleverly exploited the national feeling that a war was necessary to restore Mexican honor by announcing the need to give him money and soldiers for a war in Texas. In this way, the Texas problem became a political weapon and by his attitude Santa Anna hastened the annexation of this territory to the United States.

Hardly had Herrera's government begun when Texas applied for and obtained admission into the Union, whose Congress approved of the move without taking into account Mexico's protests refusing to acknowledge the independence of the State of Texas. Texas also intended to extend its frontiers as far as the Río Bravo and the United States supported this. Faced with this situation the Mexican minister in the United States asked for his credentials, and diplomatic relations were broken in March 1845.

With great difficulty, Herrera's government managed to equip an army of 6 thousand men to undertake the Texas campaign, and put it under the command of General Mariano Paredes Arrillaga, while the North American forces, led by General Zachary Taylor were occupying Texas and taking up position along the supposed frontier. This was the moment Paredes Arrillaga chose to use the forces which were to halt the invaders and carry off a coup d'état.

When they learned that Herrera had been overthrown, the North American forces crossed the Río Bravo to meet the Mexican army that was still waiting for the promised help. Paredes Arrillaga had himself appointed president with discretionary powers and organized a monarchical government.

The country was now definitely at war, and Mexican defeats on the northern frontier provoked a new revolution that broke out in Guadalajara on May 20, 1846. The movement was inspired by the liberal reformers headed by Gómez Farías. These reestablished the federal Constitution of 1824 and invited Santa Anna, the man of political crises, to return from exile and take charge of the government, which he did, now converted into a determined federalist.

But the country, without the means to defend itself, weakened by internal conflict, by the clumsiness of its governors and the egoism of the States that refused to supply troops and capital, was invaded by North American forces. Gómez Farías provided himself with resources by seizing Church property, but the only thing he achieved by this was a rising by the "polkos", young aristocrats who preferred to defend the interests of the clergy rather than national interests.

Gómez Farías was deposed by Santa Anna, who returned from the north when he heard of the revolt in the capital, and the order of seizure was revoked shortly after the North Americans landed in Veracruz. The invaders defeated Santa

Anna at Cerro Gordo, occupied Perote, Jalapa and Puebla, and in August 1847 arrived in the valley of Mexico, overcoming the Mexican army at Padierna, Churubusco and Chapultepec.

On September 14, the North Americans entered the capital, while Santa Anna left the country and a provisional government was installed at Querétaro. On February 2 of the following year the Treaty of Guadalupe Hidalgo was signed, by which Mexico ceded to the United States Texas, New Mexico and New California — 2 million square kilometers, more than half the territory of Mexico — against an indemification of fifteen million pesos.

The defeat caused general pessimism. The different classes began to think that Mexico was incapable of governing itself and defend itself from attacks from outside. In thirty years of independence, the country had not known either peace, economic development, social harmony or political stability.

Two governments had the task of reorganizing the nation after the war against the North Americans. José Joaquín de Herrera (1848-1849) and Mariano Ariste (1851-1852) tried to reduce and educate the army, make economies in all fields, and start important material improvements such as the building of railways and telegraphs and the introduction of electric light. Both saw their efforts hindered by the conservatives and the army leaders who felt that their interests were being threatened, the reason why these sections refused funds for the most pressing needs of the federal government.

On July 26, 1852 the Plan del Hospicio became known in Guadalajara. It was drawn up by property owners, businessmen, owners of haciendas, and clergy who did not acknowledge Arista's government and were preparing for the advent of Santa Anna's last dictatorship. Arista, without means to put down the revolt, was forced to resign.

Because of the support for the Plan del Hospicio, the rebels found it neccessary to make new arrangements and on February 4, 1853 they made the Arroyo Zarco agreements where it was decided to appoint a temporary president, the choice being Santa Anna.

Antonio López de Santá Anna was the man who even in exile could arouse in the people of Mexico the certainty that he could work miracles. On this occasion he appeared to the liberals and conservatives to be the only man capable of pulling the country out of the crisis in which it was struggling. The liberals had decided to support him, thinking that this time he would come back as a friend and supporter of civil liberties, but the conservatives succeeded in winning him over to their party by insisting that power and capital were in their hands.

In April 1853 he took up his position as dictator, composing his cabinet of prominent conservatives such as Lucas Alaman, Antonio Haro y Tamariz and Teodosio Lares. His firmest support came from the clergy, the army and the "santanistas" who allowed him to rule despotically until 1855, when dictatorial oppression caused a change of opinion about systems of government and made clear the urgent need for political and social reform.

The Reform

With Alaman's death all possibility of moderating the dictatorship through the influence of this conservative politician died. The traditional oligarchy, afraid of the reformers, was content with keeping its privileges in a certain climate of security favorable to its business. The blundering, arbitrariness and dishonesty of Santa Anna's last period reached such a degree that the Ayutla revolution was born.

It was in Guerrero that a new plan for a revolution appeared that, although it looked very similar to all the preceding ones at the beginning, was unique in that it finally succeeded in bringing about a change of people in power, the reform of the government and of Mexican society itself. When this rebellion against the abuses of Santa Anna, supported by a group of men united in the defense of their own interests, was proclaimed, it coincided with the aspirations of a great part of the nation.

At first the new rising, begun on March 4, 1854 did not arouse much unease and even the official press undertook to minimize its importance. The contents of the manifesto, apparently unimportant, united the liberals around Juan Alvarez in the hope of seeing his ideas for political, economic and social reforms realized.

The first brushes between Santa Anna's forces and the rebels showed that these were determined men, and that even though the country was tired of continual revolts, the new movement could eventually gain national support. An inevitable clash between liberals and conservatives where compromise found no place was looming up; each group's field of action became narrower and narrower until the doctrine of moderation became inapplicable in the period that was beginning.

The army was powerless to put down the rebellion in the south that was spreading to other Departments. The failure of the expeditions led by Santa Anna to fight the rebels in May 1854 and May 1855, weakened the power of the dictatorship. Ignacio Comonfort's brilliant campaigns in Michoacán, Santiago Vidaurri's triumphs in the north and the attempts at conspiracy in favor of the Ayutla Plan that were made in the capital in July 1855 finally decided the leader. He left Mexico City on August 9 and on the 18th of the same month embarked in Veracruz for Turbaco.

A few days after Santa Anna had left, there were already elements in the country opposing the revolution. On August 13 the Mexico City garrison declared in favor of the Ayutla Plan and proclaimed General Rómulo Díaz de la Vega leader. This was a bad compromise on the part of the reactionary forces, now without support, with the triumphant rebellion: they were trying to lead events in a direction false to the spirit of Ayutla. In the same month there were three more uprisings: one by Antonio Haro y Tamariz in

San Luis Potosí, one by Manuel Doblado in Guanajuato and one by Santiago Vidaurri in Nuevo León and Coahuila.

The danger of chaos being created by the division among the revolutionaries was averted by the agreements of Lagos and the diplomatic work of Comonfort. According to these agreements made on September 16, 1855, the leaders of these various movements gave up the basic conservative standpoints on ecclesiastical property and military privileges. Victory fell into the hands of the liberal group and made Ignacio Comonfort the man holding politics in balance in the new administration.

Through the Lagos agreement then, the Liberal group took control of events for the moment and was able, at least for a time, to prevent a violent clash with the conservatives. Although the election of Juan Alvarez as leader of the Ayutla revolution and temporary president did not please all the revolutionaries, his appointment was a decision dictated by the good sense of the moderate liberals. To vote out the old leader would have been to nullify the rebellion itself, that could not be considered successful until the Constitutional Congress was assembled.

Alvarez' government was unstable. The cabinet, composed of noted liberals such as Comonfort, Melchor Ocampo, Guillermo Prieto and Benito Juárez did not provide the required stability. The discontent originated not only from the conservatives whose interests were being threatened more and more, but also from the disagreement between moderate liberals who supported the conciliatory policy of Comonfort, and the radicals who were eager for more rapid changes. Unable to continue in a position that presented so many difficulties, and without means to overcome them, Juan Alvarez yielded his place to Comonfort on December 11, 1855.

The appointment of Ignacio Comonfort as substitute president was a triumph for the moderate liberals and brought hope to the conservatives. A temporary government was set up to function until a Constitution could be drawn up and some guidelines set down, but Comonfort's program was highly conciliatory. He wanted the country slowly to accept the liberal reforms put forward by his party, and his moderate politics did not satisfy anyone. For the radical liberals, he was not moving far enough; the conservatives were afraid of the continuation of reforms that would affect their interests. No conciliation was possible.

In spite of the many problems facing it, the government found itself obliged to carry out some of the reforms that the radicals desired so much, and for this reason issued various decrees that increased the fears of the conservatives. On November 23, 1855 appeared the Ley Juárez prepared by Benito Juárez to establish equality before the law; on December 28 of the same year the Ley Lafragua was promulgated that regulated the freedom of the press; and on June 25, 1856 appeared the Ley Lerdo, drawn up by Miguel Lerdo de Tejada, that ordered the disentailment of the rural and urban estates owned by civilian or ecclesiastic corporations.

The new Constitution, that raised these decrees to the rank of laws, was proclaimed on February 5, 1857 in the midst of the political unrest. New elections took place and Ignacio Comonfort was elected constitutional president, but the prospect of a new system of government did nothing to reduce the unease felt by Mexican society. The conservatives did everything they could to prevent the installation of the elected government, a division among the liberals could be foreseen, and a coup d'état by Comonfort against the directives of the Constitution was feared.

Between the beginning of September 1857 and December of the same year, there were constant uprisings to the shout of "religion and immunities (fueros)" or "constitution and reform" while the government was limited in its action by the Law.

On December 1, 1857 Comonfort legally became president and posed himself the problem of either governing according to the Constitution and thereby provoking the armed resistance of the conservatives, or else considering it invalid by its impractibility. Comonfort did not realize that it was impossible to follow a middle-of-the-road policy, that compromises were no longer acceptable and that civil war was inevitable.

On December 17, Félix Zuloaga, Comonfort's right-hand man, revolted in Tacubaya and occupied the capital without difficulty. Benito Juárez, elected vicepresident of the Supreme Court of Justice and as such, vicepresident of the country, was imprisoned together with other liberals. Ignacio Comonfort agreed with the Tacubaya Plan and the Congress, after vehement protests, ceased to function. The leader of Ayutla, supporter of moderation, had exchanged the national rank bestowed on him for that of a revolutionary.

At first the movement received the support of Veracruz, Puebla, San Luis Potosí and Tampico, and the rest of the Republic was expected to follow suit. A few days later the situation was different. On December 31, Veracruz and Tlaxcala were known to have withdrawn their support and Comonfort, believing himself lost, tried to reach the liberal coalition that had formed in the interior of the country.

On January 11, 1858 the troops of the Ciudadela, San Agustín and Santo Domingo (garrisons) in the capital rose in favor of Félix Zuloaga. Comonfort could hesitate no longer, there was nothing else to do but free Benito Juárez and hand over to him the presidency that was legitimately his.

The change brought about by the military coup at Tacubaya widened the gap between liberals and conservatives, pushing aside any idea of moderation. While the liberals were making a recovery from this turn of events to undertake the defense of the Constitution, other, politicians embraced the reactionary cause. The armed forces of both parties began at the same moment a pitiless fight: civil war.

Juárez, once at liberty, assumed the title of president and formed a liberal government that was installed in the port of Veracruz, while the conservative government, headed by Zuloaga, stayed in Mexico City.

The civil war that began came to be called the Three Year War or Reform War. The first year, 1858, was one of victory for the conservatives, won by the generals Osollo, Márquez, Mejía and Miramón, all professional military men at the head of disciplined troops, over the impovised armies of the liberal leaders Santos Degollado, Ignacio Zaragoza, Jesús González Ortega and others.

The second year, 1859, was one of triumphs for both armies, but financial difficulties for both parties. Conservatives and liberals alike needed funds to be able to continue fighting, and at first both turned to the same source: the Church. The conservatives demanded donations and forced loans, on the pretext that the clergy was the party most interested in the consolidation of the reactionary regime; the liberals based their demands first on the disentailment law of 1856 and later on the nationalization decreed by Juárez.

The civil war was destroying the labor force of the country, and at the same time any possibility of economic development. Some workers left the fields to dedicate them-

"on November 23, 1855
appeared
the Ley Juárez. . ."

selves to a more profitable activity and became bandits; the
political parties continued the struggle relentlessly and the
normal resources were exhausted. Because of this situation,
both conservatives and liberals looked abroad for the solution; the liberals turned to Europe while the conservatives,
because of their similar ideas, hoped for North American
aid.

In July 1859, almost simultaneously, the leaders of the
opposing parties announced the political programs they
intended to defend. Juárez published his on July 7 and
showed himself ready to uphold the 1857 Constitution, at
the same time announcing the separation of Church and
State. The conservative president, Miguel Miramón, who in
February of the same year had taken over from Zuloaga,
recognized in his projection of policies, dated July 12, the
need to reform the government to a certain extent but
undertook to maintain the independence and prerogatives
of the clergy. Juárez turned his projects into reality that
same month by issuing in Veracruz the Reform Laws aimed
at preventing the clergy from intervening in national politics. The forced sale of property decreed by the Ley Lerdo
had been an economic measure that only indirectly tended
to the reform of the clergy, as its main purpose was to put
into circulation and make productive the so-called "dead
hands" property. This law had not in fact taken property
away from the clergy, but since the Church continued to
foster the civil war with funds, Juárez and his group of
liberals seized its property as a political measure to prevent
its interfering in matters of State.

The law of July 12, 1859 decreed the nationalization of
Church property and established the independence of Church
and State. Other similar laws followed, designed to put an
end to the Church's great importance and the influence it

had on society. Among the most important are the one of July 23, which declared civil matrimony, the one of the 28th that established the civil registry, the one of the 31st, ordering the secularization of cemeteries, the one of August 11 that suppressed almost all religious festivities, and that of December 4 that proclaimed freedom of worship.

The Reform Laws were received enthusiastically by the liberals. The conservatives on the other hand protested strongly, declaring those people in favor of the laws to be conspirators. However, although these laws meant a movement towards a secular state, they did not, immediately at least, have the desired effects. The nationalization of Church property produced few real benefits and did not solve the financial difficulties of the liberal government.

The conservative government found itself in a similar situation. The promulgation of the Reform Laws had eliminated any possibility of truce, and the party had to pin their hopes on the military success of its leaders, Miguel Miramón and Leonardo Márquez.

Both parties realized it was urgent to bring the fight to an end to avoid foreign intervention. Agreement, then, was not possible, but funds were needed for victory, and so liberals and conservatives alike were obliged to make treaties that were damaging to the Republic in an attempt to obtain help from outside.

The conservatives made a treaty with Spain, signed on September 26 by Juan Nepomuceno Almonte for Miramón's government, and Alejandro Mon for Spain. According to this treaty, the families of Spanish subjects who had been killed at San Vicente and other places because of the civil war would be indemnified, with the sole aim of renewing relations with Spain and asking for her help in establishing a Spanish protectorate.

The liberal government made a treaty with the United States, signed on December 1, 1859 by Melchor Ocampo and Robert MacLane. The treaty involved real international easement and grave dangers for Mexican independence, granting the United States the right of traffic in perpetuity across the Isthmus of Tehuantepec in return for 4 million pesos.

As can be expected, the parties accused each other of betraying the nation, but fortunately these treaties were never put into effect. The first because it was annulled when the liberals triumphed; and the second because it was rejected by the American Senate.

The third year of the war, 1860, was favorable to the liberal cause, and towards December of that year the struggle came to an end. On December 22, Miramón fought the battle of San Miguel Calpulalpan, was defeated and retired from Mexico City, that was finally occupied on January 1, 1861 by the liberal forces of General González Ortega, while the opposing faction went into hiding only to appear a few months later at the side of the French intervention forces.

The Second Empire and the Restoration of the Republic

Juárez returned to Mexico City with his cabinet on January 11, 1861. Once established there, he ordered the expulsion of various diplomats and of some ecclesiastics who had contributed to the civil war.

The severity with which the government began its period of office was widely criticized and caused various ministerial crises. Juárez' administration was determined to uphold the 1857 Constitution and the Reform Laws, and to avoid any resurgence of the opposition. However, its real difficulties were in finance and in the necessity to carry out properly the nationalization of Church lands, a process that had been hindered and restricted by political instability and by the lack of security in the acquistion of property.

All that the Reform Laws were supposed to do — solve the finance problem, pay off the foreign debt, encourage the building of communications, subsidize colonization projects — seemed utopian dreams. The conservatives had been defeated, but not destroyed and the possibility of war remained. It was necessary to pay the armies, meet obligations contracted in the days of crisis and national land had to be sold at low prices. It was thought that under the circumstances, it was the only way of ensuring the transfer of property put forward by the Ley Lerdo. To create small properties would make the Reform irreversible, and for this reason it was done, sacrificing the present for the future.

The nation did not understand the move in this way, and only saw that the government was making a small group of speculators rich who, in return, denied their help to the government that was favoring them. The government, without Church property to sell, could only exist through loans because the customs revenues were set aside for the payment of the foreign debt, and capital was absorbed by the states. The danger of civil war could not be overlooked, ministerial crises became more and more frequent, the national deficit was approaching the sum of 5 million pesos annually, and it was almost impossible to govern.

In the middle of all this instability, the country had to prepare for elections. The Congress, in a state of political euphoria and full of dreams of instant social change, became divided into two parties in counterpoise: the pro-Juárez and the anti-Juárez factions. The presidential election was carried out without the participation of the reactionary party, that naturally abstained. The voting population chose first Miguel Lerdo de Tejada, then Benito Juárez and lastly Jesús González Ortega. Lerdo, former Minister of Finance under Juárez, was seen to be the man to organize the Reform and find a solution to the finance problem; Juárez to be a man capable because of this character to rise above the difficulties that were becoming apparent: and González Ortega to hace a program of generous revolutionary acts.

After Lerdo's death in March 1861, before the electoral process had ended, the majority of votes was for Juárez who was declared constitutional president on June 11 of the same year, with González Ortega as vicepresident.

The anti-Juárez opposition in the Congress could not prevent measures being adopted that granted Juárez extraordinary powers to save the situation, and on July 17, 1861, the extreme was reached when by decree, payment was suspended of the foreign debt for a period of two years. In fact the decree was designed to avoid bankruptcy and if the foreign creditors — French, English and Spanish — had examined the facts, they would have seen that it was the only way of putting public finance to rights, of pacifying the country and paying off the debts that had been contracted. The foreign powers however did not acquiesce and the financial problem became a more complicated international affair.

The conservatives continued to keep many groups ready to fight in all parts of the country and had started a constant guerrilla war in which they hunted down and shot the liberal leaders. Melchor Ocampo, Santos Degollado and Leandro Valle fell victims to it. While the conservative guerrillas were busy with their new fight, the political leaders of the party were negotiating for European support and the establishment of a second Empire.

The main consequence of suspending payment of the foreign debt was the so-called Tripartite Agreement. In July 1861, England, Spain and France protested against this measure and decided at the London Convention, held in October of the same year, to intervene in Mexico to obtain payment by force. The first troops disembarked in Veracruz between December 1861 and January 1862. The Mexican government entered into negociations with them and through the Treaties of La Soledad, the English and Spanish forces withdrew.

France, seeking to oppose North American expansionism with a monarchist block, stayed behind determined to impose a monarchy on Mexico and made agreements with the conservatives.

For Juárez' government the situation was discouraging. In a short time the great leaders of the revolution had disappeared: Lerdo de Tejada, Gutiérrez Zamora, Melchor Ocampo, Santos Degollado and Leandro Valle. The financial situation was not improving, and although the decree on the suspension on foreign debts had been abolished, it had not been possible to avoid French intervention. The United States was involved in a civil war and clearly could not help the liberals.

The French army and the remains of the conservative troops were commanded in succession by Generals Lorencez, Forey and Bazaine. The first was defeated at Puebla on May 5, 1862 and this decided the Mexican people to unite against him. The second general destroyed the liberal army, occupied the capital and appointed a governing junta with the job of electing the members of the Assembly of Notables and of the provisional government. Bazaine dominated almost the whole country during the French occupation, obliging Juárez and his government to establish themselves at Paso del Norte, on the border with the United States.

The conservative party, in agreement with Napoleon III, offered the crown of the Mexican Empire to Archduke Maximilian of Habsburg. He accepted the crown and promised to pay the expenses of the French intervention that reached 260 million francs. Maximilian finally reached Mexico on May 28, 1864, accompanied by his wife, the Belgian princess Charlotte Amélie (Carlota).

The establishment of an Empire satisfied the wishes and interests of the conservatives and was due to the support of the French army, but in all fairness it must be stated that Maximilian was a prince with democratic ideas and that he accepted the throne of Mexico because the conservatives who had offered it to him made him believe that it was the wish of the nation.

Juárez and the liberal party refused to acknowledge the emperor and continued the fight against him and the French, having recourse to guerrilla warfare.

Even though the military situation was favorable to him, Maximilian had to face the pressure of the clergy and the conservatives, who expected reactionary policies and the repeal of the Reform Laws. However the Emperor, because he had liberal ideas and thought that most of Mexico was liberal, accepted some reform laws and provoked the dissatisfaction of the classes that supported him.

In actual fact, his political resolutions were never put into effect. In 1866 when the American Civil War had ended, the United States pressed for the evacuation of the French and Napoleon III saw that it was necessary to withdraw the troops that supported Maximilian's empire to defend himself against Prussia. The Emperor, without the European army and supported only by conservative troops could not resist the pressure of the liberals. He surrendered in Querétaro on May 15, 1867 and was shot on the Cerro de las Campanas together with two distinguished conservative generals, Miramón and Mejía, on July 19.

The supreme political act, pardon, was up to Juárez, but he denied it. The future peace of Mexico, its absolute independence of diplomatic tutelage, the need to remove the political standard from the conservatives obliged the government of Juárez to be adamant.

With the Second Empire and the war that was officially called "War of the Second Independence", ended the long period of revolution in Mexico that began in 1810 and had been repeated in 1857. In more than half a century Mexico, because of the wars had lost more than 300 thousand inhabitants, but had won national unity. The Reform, the Republic and the Nation from then on became one and the same principle.

Juárez returned to Mexico City on July 15, 1867 to great popular enthusiasm. The empire had fallen, the conservative party annulled; the moderates, some of whom followed the empire and some the republic, had disappeared; the radical party of liberals that had carried out the Reform and beaten the French remained alone and triumphant. With his government reinstalled and free from the pressure of danger from abroad, Juárez proceeded to reorganize the country.

On August 14 new presidential elections were held to return to the constitutional system. These were all the more necessary because since November 30, 1865 Juarez' term of office as president had been at an end, but he had continued in his anomalous position by force of circumstance and the recognition of the majority of republican leaders.

This prolongation of power and the call for new elections produced a division among the liberals, and this increased because of the constitutional reforms that Juárez' government was planning. In fact, Juárez and his Minister of Justice, Sebastián Lerdo de Tejada, brother of Miguel Lerdo, thought that it was the moment to reform the Constitution, and instead of presenting the reforms before the Congress of the Union and those of the States, resorted to an illegal proceeding, using a plebiscite to win approval for such extremely important reforms as the creation of the

*"the war that was
officially called
WAR OF THE SECOND INDEPENDENCE..."*

Senate and the presidential veto of the resolutions of the Chambers.

Thus, three personalist parties were formed, that did not differ radically in their political ideas as all their representatives were liberals: the Juarists, the Lerdists and the Porfirists, the last one grouped around the figure of a new military leader, Porfirio Díaz.

After the elections Benito Juárez was declared president, with Lerdo de Tejada as vicepresident. This caused profound discontent in the country due to the pressure exerted by the government to win the elections, as Díaz was said to have had the majority of votes. The situation caused various uprisings, the most important being those of the States of San Luis Potosí, Jalisco and Zacatecas, but it is worth noting that on this occasion, none of the rebel leaders was seeking changes in the form of government. They were now asking for the observance of the Constitution, which was impossible since it was natural that the authorities should always make their candidates and ideas of government prevail now that universal suffrage had been adopted where there was a great number of landless illiterates. So Juárez, to be able to face his enemies and not violate the Constitution was forced to ask for the suspension of guarantees and extraordinary powers, by which his administration became a dictatorship with democratic leanings.

Juárez and his government were aware of the problems facing the restored Republic and took the measures they believed most effective. To revive the economy, an English company's concession was renewed to continue the building of a railway from the capital to the port of Veracruz, the only point through which international trade was carried out. The army was reorganized also, being reduced to five divisions each of 4 thousand men and political reforms were planned.

Before the end of the presidential period the supporters of Juárez began to take steps to ensure his reelection, while those who were dissatisfied with his government divided their sympathies between Lerdo de Tejada and Porfirio Díaz. The former, the true director of Juarist politics, had formed a party and put his friends in the most important posts, but was not very popular. Porfirio Díaz on the other hand, representing a younger generation that wished to take its part in national politics, had attracted public attention by his military feats in the wars of intervention and by his ability as administrator and organizer. The representatives of each man in both Chambers formed an alliance to make the opposition to Juarez' government more effective, but the president could count on a majority in the Congress that could not leave the defender of the Republic without support.

When the votes were counted, none of the candidates had the absolute majority so Congress had to elect the president. On October 12, 1871, Juárez was reappointed, and on November 8 Porfirio Díaz led an armed rebellion with the Plan de la Noria, upholding the principle of "no re-election".

The plan was supported in some parts of the country but it lost its raison d'etre when Juárez died on July 18, 1872. Taking advantage of this, the temporary president, Lerdo de Tejada issued an amnesty to all the rebels under which the only penality would be loss of military rank. Díaz refused to make use of it but, surprised in Chihuahua, had to surrender.

In the new elections for the period 1872-1876, Lerdo de Tejada was chosen constitutional president, while José María Iglesias occupied the vicepresidency. Three years later, foreseeing that President Lerdo would try for re-election in July 1876, Porfirio Díaz rose again with the Plan de Tuxtepec and again, the principle of "no re-election".

Finally, after victory over the government forces at Teocac, Díaz occupied the capital on November 23 while Lerdo went into exile in the United States. This event marked the beginning of a new era in the history of Mexico, dominated by the leader of Tuxtepec for 35 years.

Juárez' long period as president had produced a conflict between generations that was rooted not so much in differences of age or education, but in a different view of the political situation. The young politicians thought that entrance into public life was blocked by the older generation and so the only means left to them was to rise against them or wait for them to die. Their continual mutinies against Juárez and Lerdo resulted in a great desire for order and peace and the firm idea that somehow the country had to leave behind the constant crises it had lived through for more than half a century. The Porfirian regime was to bring a long period of enforced peace.

The
Porfiriato
and the
Revolution

The disappearance of Juárez from the political scene meant, although some people did not see it in this way, the disappearance of the only civilian leader capable of dominating the growing militarism. The military party had continued working in the shadows, and if it is true that circumstances obliged it to put aside its rebel attitude, it is also true that it never abandoned its plans to take over the country. The leader, General Porfirio Díaz, who had come up in the world through the struggles for the Reform and against the Intervention enjoyed well-earned prestige among his companions at arms and some fame in political circles. The triumph of the Plan de Tuxtepec placed him once again in the presidency.

Once appointed constitutional president thanks to new elections, Díaz and his collaborators, with the vague feeling that the country should be put to rights in some way or other, substituted action for ideas. They managed to force from the Congress authorization to contract for the construction of new railways, a material step forward that was given so much impulse that at the end of the Porfiriato, Mexico had a railway network of 19 thousand kilometers.

Parallel to this, postal, telegraphic and even the telephone systems were extended; harbours were constructed at Veracruz, Tampico and Salina Cruz; a series of banks were created to help and encourage agriculture, mining, commerce and industry. In 1883 the reorganization of education was begun and teachers' training colleges were founded. In 1905 the Ministry of Public Education was created and the Palace of Fine Arts begun, and in 1910 the National University was organized on modern lines. In short, the country as a whole improved its economy to an unprecedented level.

However, in social and political aspects the Porfirian regime, supported by the conservatives acted in accordance with the motto of the intellectual group called the 'scientists' —"few politics and a lot of administration", that in the long run meant an enormous division between the government and the governed. The decrees of the Reform Laws had been annulled, and the Church was again in possession of great capital and property.

The land and concessions for railways or oil drilling always harmed the peasants, who sometimes found themselves deprived of their land and without means to defend their rights. Justice and the army were always in the service of the strong, and the tiendas de raya (company stores) and the haciendas kept the peasants in a state of semi-slavery.

In addition, the rigid social stratification hindered the political rise of a new generation that felt the need to make its name in the public life of the country.

A feeling of discontent with the regime gradually developed. In spite of persecution by the authorities, political

"deprived of their land
and without means
to defend their rights. . ."

and trade-union organizations were formed. Porfirio Díaz and his group were sitting on a powder keg.

The Mexican constitution established that public offices could not be filled by re-election, but Díaz had changed these articles to make sure of remaining in power. In the early years of the 20th century the liberal movement that condemned these changes affirmed itself and a young landowner, Francisco I. Madero, published a book entitled 'The Presidential Sucession of 1910', in which he censured the evils of militarism, studied various national problems that the Porfirian government had been unable to solve, and ended by asking for the return of the principle of 'no re-election' that had been wielded by Díaz himself as a weapon against Juárez and Lerdo de Tejada.

The truth was that from 1904 on, Mexican society had been asking who would succeed Díaz as president, who was by this time very old and possibly with little time left to live. His last re-election at the age of 80, did nothing to solve the problem of the presidential succession.

In the 1910 presidential elections, Díaz emerged triumphant once again, thanks to the fraud practiced by government agents. The liberals, who had supported Francisco I. Madero's candidature, then formulated the Plan de San Luis, declaring these elections invalid. On November 20 revolution broke out throughout the country, supported by armed bands that later became the very soul of the revolutionary army. The guerrilla chiefs Pascual Orozco, Francisco Villa and Emiliano Zapata made their names famous at this time.

Chihuahua was the scene of defeats of Porfirian troops: Ciudad Guerrero, Mal Paso, Casas Grandes, Chihuahua, Ciudad Juárez were the battles that opened up the way to the revolutionaries. Having failed in both military ventures and

*"revolution broke out
throughout
the country. . ."*

in negotiations, Díaz resigned, and left the country in May 1911.

Madero at the head of the triumphant revolution, took over as president on November 6, but, being a man with a romantic ideal of democracy, liberty and tolerance, he was not qualified to stand up to the opposition of the Porfirians or to the impatience of his own partisans, for whom to compromise was to liquidate the revolution.

From the beginning there were risings of opposing factions throughout the country, putting into relief the fact that the differences sprang from something more than just politics. Old and bitter issues such as the owning of land took on great importance, and those who suffered were of the opinion that the revolution should satisfy them immediately.

In addition, the fighting had not touched the social and economic organization of the Porfirian world. The climate of insecurity motivated the holders of economic power and the representatives of foreign interests, supported by the embassy of the United States and allied with the Porfirian army, to use General Victoriano Huerta to seize power and assassinate Madero on February 22, 1913.

Victoriano Huerta began a reign of terror during which the liberals were persecuted mercilessly. In reaction to this dictatorship, and in the face of Madero's death, the revolutionaries rallied round General Venustiano Carranza and proclaimed the Plan de Guadalupe with the purpose of restoring constitutional order, interrupted by the Huerta coup.

To the already well-known names of Villa and Zapata, were added those of Obregón, Pesquieira, Diéguez, Hill and other men who with victories such as those at Torreón, Orendain and Tepic overcame the resistance of Huerta.

Huerta, defeated in all parts, went into exile in July 1914.

Carranza, the new leader, had an acute instinct for politics. He dissolved the Porfirian army and tried to build a government capable of carrying out any social and economic changes necessary, but the urgency to solve the agrarian problem made this a hopeless task. Also, the ambitions of the new "caudillos" endangered Carranza's position.

Two conventions were held, in Mexico City and at Aguascalientes to solve the conflicts among the revolutionaries, but the only result in fact was a complete break in revolutionary unity. Villa and Zapata became enemies of Carranza and Obregón, and began a new fight that ended in the battle of Celaya from which constitutionalism, represented by the Carranza faction, emerged triumphant.

With the differences apparently solved, and with a new Constitution drawn up in 1917, Carranza was the first to govern under the new constitutional system. But the social revolution was going slowly, and the president considered that the allotted period of four years was not long enough for great changes to be made. As the moment for a change of power came closer, he tried to prolong his period of government through a civilian candidate, Ignacio Bonilla; at this point, the revolutionaries began to quarrel among themselves once more and Carranza's hopes were destroyed. The fight between the civilian Carranza and General Alvaro Obregón came to an end when Carranza was assassinated on May 1, 1920.

In 1920, after a short civilian regime Obregón, one of the most brilliant and powerful military leaders that the revolutionary movement had produced, became president. The following year, supported by the middle class, he began the rebuilding of the nation. He initiated the agrarian reform by prohibting the 'latifundio' (large landed estate) and promoting small properties and the 'ejido' (semi-communal lands) thereby building a more complex and productive economy and making the redistribution of land a guarantee of the industrialization of the nation.

At the same time, the distribution of land awakened in the peasants an attitude of hope that, used skillfully for political ends, brought about their alliance with the State. A similar process was to follow in the case of the workers, profiting from the fact that the labor movement, because it was weak, had always in the final instance looked to the State for the protection of its interests against employers.

In this way the State acquired two powerful forces for socio-political action whose effectiveness was proved at the peaceful transfer of power to General Plutarco Elías Calles in 1924.

At the end of Calles' term of office, there were many other signs of the change happening in the country. Mexico was definitely entering the era of transformation that would give it the right to figure as a modern nation. Continuity in power allowed the governing group to have a hand in other forms of social control. When complementary measures for economic change were effected, the dispersal of property encouraged the growth all over the country of a class that was economically strong and did not exclusively form part of the government.

The type of leadership represented in its final form by Obregón and Calles would disappear through the social forces that they themselves created. From this time on, political power was institutionalized and Mexico entered a new stage of modern development.

Present Days

The government of President Calles laid the foundations of modern Mexico; the central bank — the Bank of Mexico, S.A. — already anticipated by the 1917 Constitution was created, and economic legislation was strengthened through various laws such as that on credit institutions and that on agricultural credit, necessary for the progress of the country. The creation of the social and economic infrastructure was begun on a firm basis with the establishment of the National Highways Commission and the National Irrigation Commission. Internal peace was assured and from this time on, except for the bitter religious struggle, the revolutionary regime's institutionalism was asserted.

The assassination of the president, General Alvaro Obregón on July 17, 1928, whose reelection had been possible due to a constitutional reform, legally brought Emilio Portes Gil to the presidency of the Republic. His main, almost only goal was to call the elections in which Ortiz Rubio was elected president, to take up his post on February 5, 1930.

The most important act of Ortiz Rubio's government, who was not to terminate his period of office as he resigned on September 3, 1932, was to formulate the Estrada Doctrine according to which Mexico does not announce recognition of de facto governments, as this could go against the principle of Non-intervention. In such cases Mexico simply either maintains or recalls its diplomats, whichever is considered suitable, without passing judgement on the legitimacy of the new government, a decision that is exclusively the concern of the nation involved. This measure, together with the Calvo Doctrine, that determines the formal renunciation of one the parties from diplomatic intervention in the case of dispute, are considered to be Latin America's most important contributions to modern international law.

When Ortiz Rubio resigned from his position of President of the Republic he was succeeded by General Abelardo L. Rodríguez who held power from September 1932 to November 1934.

On December 1, 1934 General Lázaro Cárdenas took over as President and, through a reform of the Constitution, held office for six years — formerly the president's term of office had been four — during which time the most significant events were the impetus given to agrarian reform and, above all, the expropriation of the oil industry, that made the subsoil the property of the nation. It was during General Cárdenas' presidency that the last revolution headed by General Saturnino Cedillo, occurred in 1938.

Cárdenas was succeeded by General Manuel Avila Camacho (1940-1946) who in home affairs distinguished himself by social legislation, exemplified by the law that created the Mexican Institute of Social Securiy (1934). In the sphere of international politics, president Avila Camacho had to face the situation created by aggression to Mexican oil tankers that led to the declaration of a state of war between Mexico and the Axis powers.

Miguel Alemán took over from Avila Camacho as president on December 1, 1946 and held office until November 30, 1952. This period of government is noted for the impetus given to economic activity that advanced the country along the road of development.

He was followed as president by Adolfo Ruiz Cortines, from December 1, 1952 to November 30, 1958. During this period, the country continued to develop and one of the most important acts of this government was the granting of votes to women, implicit in the 1917 Constitution.

Ruiz Cortines was succeeded by Adolfo López Mateos, who held office from December 1, 1958 to November 30, 1964. During this administration great advances were made in child protection and in the country's foreign relations. In international affairs, one of the most important achievements of president López Mateos was the definitive solution of the El Chamizal problem through the return to Mexico of this territory by the United States, after it had been recognized as belonging to Mexico by a court of arbitration. In home affairs, president López Mateos instituted the system of party deputies, a step towards improving the democracy. In the field of economy should be mentioned the nationalization in 1960 of electricity.

Gustavo Díaz Ordaz took over from president López Mateos on December 1, 1964 and his term of office finished on November 30, 1970. During this period the 1968 Olympic Games were held in Mexico.

President Díaz Ordaz handed over power to Luis Echeverría Alvarez on December 1, 1970. President Echeverría proposed and obtained the adoption by the United Nations Organization the Carta de los Derechos y Deberes Económicos de los Estados (Charter of the Economic Rights and Duties of Nations), a statute defending the rights and progress of Third World Countries.

The present president, José López Portillo, succeeded president Echeverría Alvarez on December 1, 1976 and his term of office will come to an end on November 30, 1982. He was immediately faced with the crisis caused by the devaluation of the peso in August 1976. The economy is firmly on the way to recovery through the exploitation of all the country's resources to help in the continuing evolution of the Mexican nation.

Other titles in the **PANORAMA** series

HISTORY

ARCHAEOLOGY AND ANTHROPOLOGY

ART

POPULAR ART

Other titles in the **PANORAMA** series

TRADITIONS

MEN AND HORSES OF MEXICO
José Alvarez del Villar

TITLES BEING PREPARED

INDIAN COSTUMES OF MEXICO
Ruth D. Lechuga

Printed by:
Editora de Periódicos, S.C.L.
La Prensa
División Comercial
Prolongación de Pino 577
Col. Arenal 02980 México, D.F.
3000 copies
Mexico City September 1985